Van Graves

Discovering The Pennines

DISCOVERING THE
PENNINES

VAN GREAVES

The Crowood Press

First published in 1991 by
The Crowood Press Ltd
Ramsbury,
Marlborough
Wiltshire SN8 2HR

British Library Cataloguing in Publication Data

Greaves, Van
    Discovering the Pennines.
    1. England. Travel. Mountains
    I. Title
    914.2804859

ISBN 1 85223 132 7

Picture Credits

All maps and colour photographs by the author. Original prints from these
pictures can be ordered from the author (tel: 021 422 1621).

Typeset by Chippendale Type Ltd., Otley, West Yorkshire.
Printed and bound by Times Publishing Group, Singapore.

CONTENTS

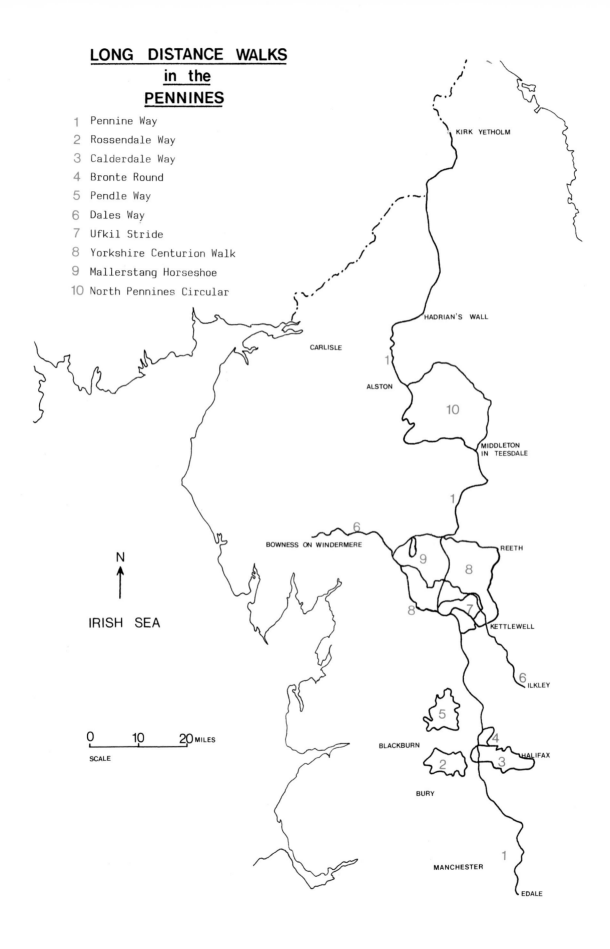

LONG DISTANCE WALKS
in the
PENNINES

1 Pennine Way
2 Rossendale Way
3 Calderdale Way
4 Bronte Round
5 Pendle Way
6 Dales Way
7 Ufkil Stride
8 Yorkshire Centurion Walk
9 Mallerstang Horseshoe
10 North Pennines Circular

N

IRISH SEA

0   10   20 MILES

SCALE

KIRK YETHOLM

HADRIAN'S WALL

CARLISLE

ALSTON

10

MIDDLETON
IN TEESDALE

1

6

BOWNESS ON WINDERMERE

9

8

REETH

8

7

KETTLEWELL

6 ILKLEY

5

4

BLACKBURN

2

3 HALIFAX

BURY

MANCHESTER

1

EDALE

INTRODUCTION

Somewhere, exactly where is a point of contention, the Midland Plain gives way to a notable rise in land, an uplifting billowing swell of terrain characterized by moorland and dales. This upland surely defines the beginnings of the north of England, vast quantities of which lie above 300m (1,000ft), much above 450m (1,500ft) and acres on, around or above 600m (2,000ft). This landscape continues almost unabated to the Scottish border country. As we are privileged by the use of language to name places of all kinds, we named these uplands the Pennines. Physically, climatically, and economically they provide an altogether unique character. In the economical sense, they could almost be accused of bounding the now politically popular theme of the North/South divide. Conditions all round are bleaker here, colder, windier, wetter. Life just seems to be that much tougher in the Pennines. Many of the buildings are of thick stone, squat, huddling, each protective towards its neighbour. At times, the Pennines can be utterly dreary. However, the friendliness within these hills is second to none, and it is equalled by the wonderful cheer of a bright sunny day when the hills stretch away under blue skies decked with soft white clouds that create the feeling of an ability to see forever.

A lover of classical mountains has the need to visit the Pennines several times before he convinces himself that they are more than a meaningless sprawl of endless whalebacks. Their flanks are decorated with gritstone and limestone rock outcrops, the former, black, forbidding and engendering to some, a feeling of austerity. Indeed, Alfred Wainwright, of Lakeland fame, although foraging into the Pennines to write his *Pennine Way Companion* (Westmorland Gazette), which I recom-

mend along with his *Coast to Coast Walk* (Westmorland Gazette), will surely be interpreted as greatly preferring his Lakeland mountains to the Pennines, even though he sings the praises of the Limestone country around the Three Peaks of Yorkshire, Whernside, Ingleborough and Penyghent in his book, *Walks in Limestone Country* (Westmorland Gazette). In spite of this, have you ever seen his writings on Gritstone country? I think not. Gritstone country however, is the perfect foil for the brighter, more serene limestone dales and hills. These two rock types in the main form separate hills. However, in places they can be juxtaposed, and are often seen one overlaying the other on some bare hillside, in fact very occasionally you will see one (the gritstone) lying on top of the other (limestone), as at Norber near Austwick – some excellent examples of glacial erratics. Gritstone moors are more associated with peat hags, acid soils, thick tussocky grasses and weird weathered rock formations. Limestone walking is generally dry over neat pastures, some superb pavements, ravines, gorges, by cliffs, caves, and often along dales. The Pennines can be described as 'chalk and cheese' country with a landscape to arouse most emotions.

Geographically, we can argue where the Pennines start. I have no quibble with the Pennine Way starting its long course at Edale. It is easily reached by public transport from Manchester or Sheffield, or by car from many areas. However, can you really say the Pennines start here? Edale is a fine wide dale but south of it the hills continue for many a kilometre. Alfred Wainwright suggests he would start the Way at Dovedale near Ashbourne: 'a grand entrance through a classical limestone dale'. He would finish the walk at Hadrian's

Wall. Personally, I put hills in preference to dales and I would start a Pennine Way at Hen Cloud and The Roaches near Leek, Staffordshire. These fine sentinels are a justifiable barrier to the lowland in the south. So this alternative would then go via Gradbach, either Shutlingsloe, a super mini-mountain, or via Three Shires Head to Shining Tor, then through Hayfield over to Kinder Downfall to rejoin the original Way. Possibilities exist for a diversion at Laddow Rocks on Black Hill over to Chew Reservoir and the fine gritstone edge of Saddleworth Moor to Diggle and then again on the normal Way at Standedge. The route could break off once more at Blackstone Edge to descend to Calderbrook, then over to Cornholme and traverse Black Hameldon Hill to Trawden and Earby. At Thornton-in-Craven the original route is rejoined all the way to Hadrian's Wall, where I, too, would finish.

It is my contention that the nature of the countryside changes here. The Pennines are lost to forests and the Cheviot Hills are still distant and are more related to the Scottish Southern Uplands. There then comes the problem of the Peak District. Having stated that topographically, the Pennines start at the southern end of the Peak District, a decision has to be made about their relationship to this long-established and well-defined area. Because of the Peak District's complexity, its own identification as a national park, and the vast amount of literature already available on the area (in particular for the walker), the Peak District, except for areas involving the Pennine Way or the suggested alternative is too cumbersome to include.

We must now further define the Pennine areas. In order to explore them, I have collared various walks (almost all of them circular), which circumnavigate all of the quite naturally defined districts of the Pennine chain. To become attuned to the countryside can be no better achieved than to backpack for several days from place to place with a tent or more comfortable accommodation over your head from youth hostel to guest house to hotel or inn. Nevertheless, some day or half-day wanderings are mentioned sometimes in association with these longer outings, sharing part of their route or if not then at least situated nearby. This book is not designed to be a step by step guide to walks. Step by step guides are available and will be referenced. The maps herein are simplistic. Let this book rather lay down the bait for you to take its content and advice, thus encouraging you to sort out your own walk, or potter, by researching further, the references provided.

North of the High Peak lies an area now mapped as the South Pennines. To its west, the hills stretch out a shoulder into east Lancashire actually signposted on roads as The Western Pennines. Two treks and one ascent are chosen to explore this district. First, the Rossendale Way. This is a 70-km (45-mile) circular walk covering the rather unfashionable moorland bounding the Borough of Rossendale; unfashionable because it is mainly an area frequented by locals rather than tourists from distant parts. Because this trek is next in a northerly progression of this book, does not mean it comes second in preference to the Pennine Way, rather, we are moving in a logical northerly direction along the Pennine chain. The Rossendale Way is bounded by the towns of Bury, Haslingden, Rawtenstall, Bacup, Accrington, and Oswaldtwistle, names which conjure up for me a feeling of 'clog country'. For reasons which may become apparent in the section on this walk, I would advise newcomers to the Pennines only to include this in their itinerary, after several other areas have been explored.

Adjacent to this area, wholly in Lancashire and within the borough of Pendle is the recent innovation of the Pendle Way. This is a 72-km (45-mile) circular walk, signposted with the very relevant witches on their broomsticks. The very varied and pretty countryside encountered throughout this trek includes an ascent of Pendle Hill, which is 'out on a limb' from the Pennine chain.

The Calderdale Way is a 80-km (50-mile) circular walk encapsulating all that is West Yorkshire. It cleverly avoids much of the surrounding urban development, weaving a line over moors, deep valleys, pasture, across causey stones, near to fine examples of mills with surviving chimney stacks, canals and basins and a passage through Brighouse Town. Hebden Bridge and Heptonstall are encountered as well as Todmorden. Calderdale Metropolitan Borough Council have done much to improve the once dingy industrial legacy of the Calder Valley and environs, turning them into a now advantageous tourist facility. If desired, it is possible to link the Calderdale and Rossendale Ways.

The walk known popularly as the Brontë Round, 37km (23 miles), is worth an outing, preferably split at Haworth to allow some exploration of this town with its obvious historical connections. There will be no problem getting a meal in this area because there are many good fish and chip shops in the South Pennines.

By far the most popular area of the Pennines are the Yorkshire Dales. Our explorations of this superb walking area begin with the Dales Way and linked day or half-day walks. The Dales Way is well documented, but it is a fine introduction to backpacking in the dales, which are as much moors and fells as valleys. However, the route here generally keeps a lower profile, following valley floors to create a linear walk. The true way only crosses one real fell, Cam Fell, but I have suggested an ascent of Great Knoutberry Fell as an alternative way into beautiful Dentdale. I've also picked out a walk in Dentdale and Deepdale which shares part of the Yorkshire Dales Centurion Walk.

If you are willing and able to cover 53km (33 miles) of the best of Yorkshire Dales scenery within one tough day, then the Ufkil Stride can be shared with annual eventers in June or by careful arrangement with a car-driver-cum-checker any other time. Experienced walkers could do it alone, however, this is a cue to remind everyone of the inherent risks involved in being unaccompanied in wild country. The walk is officially based on Buckden village but I would prefer to start and finish at Arncliffe. Further walking in this district must include Malham, Gordale Scar, Malham Tarn, Malham Lings and Malham Cove with more possibilities around Buckden Pike or Mastiles Lane, a classic green lane.

One of the finest backpacking trips perhaps anywhere in England is to experience the Yorkshire Dales Centurion Walk, approximately 160km (100 miles) around many of the outer fells of the national park, taking in the Three Peaks of Ingleborough, Whernside and Penyghent, Dentdale, The Howgill Fells from Sedburgh to Ravenstonedale, Smardale, sharing part of the Coast to Coast Walk via Kirkby Stephen to Nine Standards Rigg. A rough moorland crossing to Tan Hill, Britain's highest inn is followed by more of the same over Arkengarthdale Moor, into Arkengarthdale and Reeth, (with suggested alternatives). From Reeth it goes to Aysgarth in Wensleydale, then Buckden Pike and Great Whernside before a return to the start at Horton in Ribblesdale is effected via Littondale and Penyghent.

No exploration of the Yorkshire Dales would be complete without walks in two of its most famous dales, Wensleydale and Swaledale and I have included some suggestions. To conclude the Dales, two walks in Nidderdale are included, not within the national park, but equal competitors with those within its boundaries. As the limestone country of the Craven district is so delectable, its finer points need to be explored. A walk in Crummackdale via Norber Erratics is highly recommended. This dale seems strangely quiet, serene, and free from tourists. It has two virtual canyon-style rims of limestone and scars that are lunar in design. It has a real wilderness feel to it with Moughton, Penyghent and Ingleborough as backcloths. Indeed, at Norber (the walk's entry point), gritstone erratic boulders can be found lying on top of younger limestone clints.

Further possibilities of limestone walking include Attermire Scar above Settle and the smooth sculptured pavements beneath Ingleborough, Scar Close and Southerscales being national nature reserves. The other side of the Doe river contains Twisleton Scar and Scales Moor. These finely honed limestone structures are not for heads down and footslogging, they are for quietly pottering and gazing, taking in their unique designs, looking for the rare flora and for meditating upon. They are a delight to experience before entering one of Ingleton's detectable 'Glens'.

An ascent of Wild Boar Fell in the Mallerstang Valley can be included for its own sake, or as part of the Mallerstang/ Nine Standards Yomp, an annual walkers event raising much money for charity. This fine fell has a steep scarped face overlooking the Mallerstang Valley, and indeed from that side, thrusts up quite a mountainous facade.

What remains of the Pennines after the Yorkshire Dales? A vast area, wild, unspoilt, in many parts infrequented and arguably neglected, save for the Pennine Way country of the Tees watershed and the Cross Fell area. It awaits those who wish to venture on to lonelier hills. And hill country it is. It is dissected by some of the highest roads in England, has many 600m (2,000ft) tops and contains remote valleys and settlements. It does not enjoy popularity, being as it is, that much more distant from urban conurbations than the more southerly Dales and Pennines. My wife and I walked a circular backpacking route in these hills, which are referred to as the Northern Pennines. We bought maps including the 1:25,000 Teesdale and the Allenheads and Allendale Town/ Rookhope which were very good, from the ordinary 1:25,000 series. We then based a walk on Middleton-in-Teesdale, taking in the Pennine Way from there to Alston then via Ninebanks to Allendale

Town, from there on to Rookhope in Upper Weardale, Eastgate and/or Stanhope, Catterick Moors, Bollihope Common, Monks Moor and finally returning to Middleton. This is a wild walk, taking between 5 days and a week, however, it was well accommodated at the necessary points.

As a day outing, Cross Fell can be ascended for its own sake as the highest point in the Pennines, starting from Kirkland in the Eden Valley. A neighbouring walk beginning from Murton up Hilton Fell, Maize Beck, High Cup Nick (that little Grand Canyon of the Pennines) and Dufton gives a bracing outing in good fells and moorland, that includes the grandeur of High Cup Nick.

The A689 is the highest major road in England at 627m (2,057ft) and ways are possible over trackless, but walkable fells such as Burnhope Seat or Killhope Law. Finally, at the point where I maintain the Pennines rather peter out, comes the more frequented Hadrian's Wall which follows a natural ridge with commanding positions, that were most necessary in the days of the Romans. It affords a fine finale to this Pennine sojourn, with topographical features to lure the walker, and the inevitable amateur historian has the several Roman remains to explore.

I have tried to put together in this book what is otherwise fragmented information. I'm sure people want to know, in the most convenient way possible, what the Pennines can offer. There are so many places, innumerable to mention, that have had to be excluded, but they would require a book of encyclopaedic proportions, or several volumes to cover them completely. Then is it complete?

The possibilities are never ending, so what we have put together here is a taster, a logical series of walks to cover strategic areas of the Pennines, and the lie of the land revealed through the pictures. This will hopefully be followed by actual encounter, so that in the end you can surely say that you explored the Pennines and discovered there are many Pennine Ways.

Notes on Walking and Weather

The nearest anything comes to mountainous in the Pennines is Penyghent, Ingleborough or Wild Boar Fell, where their flanks are rocky and quite sheer. Elsewhere, the ascents or descents in the Pennines are gradual, sometimes longwinded. It is the nature of the terrain underfoot, particularly the peaty and spongy gritstone areas which tax the keenest and fittest of walkers. Even pottering around limestone pavements is potentially dangerous with their greasy sometimes slimy surfaces. I've slipped a few times just taking a simple step! (But maybe that was after the lunch visit to the pub!)

What makes the Pennines challenging is their lack of protection from the elements. In bad weather, a long moorland crossing without shelter would have you swap it at the drop of a hat for a higher, yet leaward shelter on some Snowdonia, Lakeland, or Scottish mountain ridge. I am also personally convinced that it rains more in the Pennines than many other places, for instance Wales! However, the western districts may be cloud-covered, whilst more eastern areas may see more broken cloud and sunny intervals. Also note that the Pennine Way is probably more dangerous to your health in a heat wave, than in misty, wet or windy conditions. Be prepared for anything and take a small first aid kit. I personally burst my blisters, then I plaster 'em! I take embrocation cream for multi-day backpacking trips, and I'm not averse to walking in trainers in good weather and drier conditions.

For beginners, perhaps do the day or half-day walks in this book before the multi-day treks. Learn to use a map and compass. Most people find it a reasonable task. Follow the Country Code in all ways. I still ask at farms if in doubt as to the way through them. Take a well-designed rucksack without 'the kitchen sink' in it! Preferably take Goretex waterproof clothing . . . no sweat!

Finally, I've tried to keep to rights of

way throughout. Any mistakes are purely unintentional.

Notes on Photography

I use Nikon 35mm cameras and independent manufacturers' lenses, particularly Vivitar and Sigma, which I recommend. A 28–105 vari-focal lens is all that is basically required by the walking photographer, though I do take a 70–300 zoom lens at times and a 24mm wide angle gives that much more width than a 28mm. I would take a compact 35mm zoom camera if I was only using colour print film; it's very handy, very light and accurate enough for prints in the auto mode. However, much more control and experience is required with transparency films (of which Fujichrome is my favourite stock). This is because many 'compacts' lack the over-riding facilities on a 35mm SLR and transparency film has less latitude, that is less range tolerance to acceptable exposures than colour negative film.

For black and white, you should generally note the observations on colour, though again only much experience will help you to determine how to expose it if you are developing and printing it yourself. If you can, take a tripod to photograph low light conditions, super results being gained by those prepared to do this either very early or late in the day.

Finally, take pictures in the first place for your own enjoyment, but if you are concerned with others' criticism, take a long hard look at what your picture conveys. There are too many rules and non-rules of composition to go into here, so ask yourself if your picture has a real meaning to a viewer who has never been to its location. If it has, you are on the way to using your photographs to communicate to others, which is precisely what photography sets out to achieve.

Chapter 1

THE PENNINE WAY –
SOUTHERN EXTENSION

Maps	OS Peak District Tourist: 1 inch to 1 mile. Two maps from the 1:25,000 series covering the White and Dark Peak. The walk is a southern link to the official Pennine Way from Hen Cloud, (Staffordshire Moorlands) to the Kinder Plateau. It is 1½ days walking and the distance is approximately 35km (22 miles).
Transport	There are rail services to Stoke-on-Trent and Buxton. The bus service X23 goes from Sheffield and Hanley and you alight at Blackshaw Moor or Upper Hulme. Tel: 0298 3098
Accommodation	Meerbrook Youth Hostel, 0538 34244; Keekorak Lodge Farm, Upper Hulme, 0538 34218; Gradbach Mill Youth Hostel, 0260 227625; Mrs Wyatt, Tunstead Guest House, Kinder, Hayfield, 0663 42138. There are campsites at Upper Hulme, 0538 34202 and Hayfield, 0663 45394. You can get other information via Peak Park Planning Board, 0629 814321.

PENNINE WAY   SOUTHERN EXTENSION

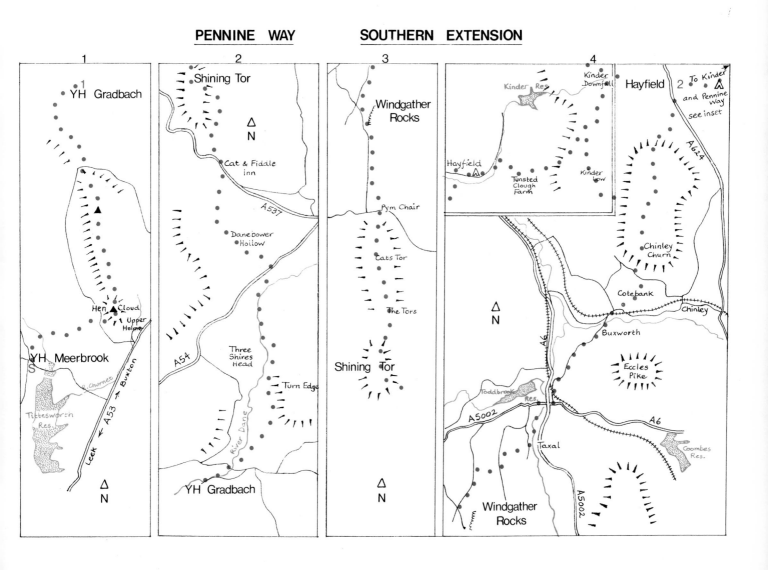

Proceeding in a northerly direction from the Staffordshire Moorlands town of Leek, the A53 road to Buxton soon reveals an upward moorland swell to the right. The eye, however, will be drawn ahead left where there appears a veritable fortress of a hill, bearing large split buttresses and a castellated skyline. Although, travelling from the south has for some kilometres gently given rise to upland, no more so than here does it put forth its barrier. The hill is Hen Cloud, behind it, the spiky point of Ramshaw Rocks and further left the serrated edge of the Roaches. Nowhere to the south has the landscape provided such a gesture. The gesture says, 'this is real hill country, and you are entering upon it'.

There is no mention of the Pennines here, either in area signs or names on the map. The Peak District National Park has its boundary here, but the Pennine Way does not start officially until 32 kilometres to the north. Through the years, no one has really referred to the hills above as the start of the Pennine chain. The way areas have been designated means that you do not encounter the name 'Pennines' until you reach the M62 motorway which is just included in the 1:25,000 series entitled 'South Pennines'. The Pennine Way starts in the heart of the High Peak and another 30 kilometres or so are required to reach the South Pennines map. But here we are, 64 kilometres to the south of anywhere denoted 'Pennines'. However, to a studier

of topography or geology, the Pennine hills first manifest themselves beyond Leek and these characteristics continue virtually unabated northwards.

Therefore, with this starting point in mind, and such a fine area of country lying before Edale, you will not regret walking a day and a half's extension to the south to start perhaps with an overnight stay at Meerbrook Youth Hostel or by being dropped off at the foot of Hen Cloud. Indeed, there are people who visit the Roaches on innumerable occasions because its collection of rocks, its elevated ridge and the extended vistas, all comprise its magnetism.

Visitors to this area, can easily walk on to the ridge, though Hen Cloud is a pull.

Hen Cloud, a gritstone fortress in the Staffordshire moorlands.

Hen Cloud and the Roaches (Staffs Moorlands) give access to country that is Pennine in character.

Ramshaw Rocks is a weird collection flanking the A53 and another easy walk leads over its edge where exploration can be made of the eroded pinnacles on or below them depending which side you are on. The aim is, however, to walk from Hen Cloud to Gradbach Mill Youth Hostel. Nimble walkers can get up Hen Cloud directly between the buttresses, otherwise the hill is skirted leftward to double back up the short ridge to the summit rocks, to peer if you dare over the precipices frequented by rock climbers. Turning sights towards the Roaches, a dip is crossed through a gate in a stone wall. The choice is up and round the back of the ridge or underneath the Upper Tier of the Roaches where it might be possible to watch climbers at play, dangerous looking play, particularly if the ascent of Sloth, the main

On the Roaches near Roach End with Shutlingsloe beyond.

Gradbach Mill Youth Hostel.

crack in the large overhang of the tallest buttress is being attempted. Don Whillans and Joe Brown first ascended this in the 1950s. Today, it still represents a mental and physical test for aspiring hard men. Beyond the main buttress, the ground eases and there is a definite way up on to the ridge, whereby the route proceeds.

The next notable feature is Doxy's Pool, an unusually rare gritstone tarn suspended on the moorland levels. Below, the conifer woods once sheltered a yak and wallabies that escaped from a zoo. Strange, but true! In the summer of 1989, with my son Rick, we encountered a wallaby browsing on the heather-clad slopes of Black Tor some fifty metres off to the left of the Pennine Way north of

Crowden. I'm not joking! It really was a wallaby! There are wallabies in the Peak District!

Back to Doxy's Pool. Doxy was a beautiful girl with a voice to match. She sang in an unknown tongue, so the story goes, on summer evenings on the Roaches. She was carried off by strange men, but left a ghost, the 'Singing Woman of the Roaches', who walks the ridge on dark nights.

This skyline walk continues until a gradual rise culminates at the trig point on the Roaches summit at over 450m (1,500ft). Hill and moor stretch in most directions, as a descent through a collection of wind-eroded rocks reveals the fine mini-mountain of Shutlingsloe ahead. It is a hill worthy of ascent. It is a shame it is too

circuitous a walk to include it in this journey. Though, it is feasible to do it as an alternative, staying overnight in the environs of Langley, then following the Gritstone Trail and seeking departure from it in order to end up at Windgather Rocks.

At Roach End find the trail left of a stone wall that goes down a heathery moor towards Gradbach Wood. Entering this provides a sylvan contrast to the bleakness of before, as the trail goes down to the Black Brook, home of dippers and visited by herons. Turn right over the footbridge in a delightful situation to follow a broad trail to Gradbach Mill Youth Hostel.

The youth hostel is an historical building originating around 1640. Around 1785 it burned down and the existing mill was erected, having a 7-m (24-ft) diameter wheel. It was offered for sale about 1837. A short historical void occurred, then during the 1850s it produced flax and silk. It ceased production in 1862 and was neglected until 1885 when Sir John Harpur Crewe used it as a saw mill, for his large estate. It then devalued to use as a barn, the mill pond being adapted for water cress beds. These in turn disappeared and in the 1950s the huge water wheel was sold for scrap. In 1977, the Harpur Crewe estate offered the site for sale. The YHA bought and converted the property to its present use. A more charming overnight location could not be wished for.

Day 2 departs from Gradbach to follow the Dane Valley into its upper reaches. Start by taking the hostel drive to the road and turning left, or take a footbridge to Manor Farm. The River Dane flows down to the left as five enclosures are traversed. The views open out behind with the Roaches rising above the cloak of woodland, but in front the valley is seen to become confined by enroaching hillsides. A walled unmetalled lane levels out to reach the pack horse bridges at Three Shires Head, the meeting place of Staffordshire, Cheshire and Derbyshire county boundaries. The final approach sees the Dane River flow through a small gorge where rowan trees wrinkle out between the small precipices. Although this place seems very cut off, there is often someone there picnicking, paddling or snoozing on the river bank. The main bridge over the Dane is crossed to proceed on the other bank into ever wilder environs. At a ruined building, the Dane, now a moorland stream, is left below as a climb is made to the A54 passing a chimney on the right. A fifty-metre road walk finds a wide but easily missed grass track up to Danebower Hollow. It is hardly a hollow, as the path rises to give extensive views towards Shutlingsloe and Sutton Hill, even the Cheshire plain beyond. Shutlingsloe's turret draws the eye and beckons a future visit to its summit, but for now the moorland path dips over a pass to reveal the famous Cat and Fiddle Public House straight ahead on the level moor. It may be lunchtime by now and a pint with your sandwiches might not go amiss. If you're like me, the effect of a lunchtime pint makes the restart all the

Three Shires Head, the meeting of Staffordshire, Derbyshire and Cheshire.

Towards Shining Tor.

Windgather Rocks.

Abseiling, Windgather Rocks

On Chinley Hill above Hayfield.

Edale Valley in winter.

more woozy! Having got into gear, the stone path down the road is taken revealing an old milestone – 'London 164 miles'. Keep right at first but turn left at a ladder stile to follow the footpath to Pym Chair. It can be boggy here until the rising ground drains the wet and arrival is made on to Shining Tor, at 511m (1,677ft). The trig point is accessible by a stile and is on private ground. There follows a bracing moorland walk, Pennine in character, following the backbone of the upland, passing Cats Tor and reaching the road at Pym Chair. Although the Goyt Valley is parallel, the reservoirs are out of sight in the dip, but Shutlingsloe has still kept its now conical looking summit in retrospect all the way. The road or at first moorland track can be followed to Windgather Rocks,

another rock climbers' playground. The way ahead over Taxal Moor gives views towards Kinder Scout. Before embarking upon it, care is required just past the five ways junction, in order to find the correct path off right. Bear right rather than sharp right and cross the moor. Find the minor road and go leftwards to a ladder stile. Once this is crossed, the way to Taxal is obvious. Turn left again by the Chimes of Taxal where a path leads to the A5002 Buxton road. Finding the Jolly Roger Inn, go left along Old Road and head for Buxworth which nestles in an industrial looking valley. The idea is to ascend out of Buxworth under the railway via Cotebank to a lane. A few metres left of this, a walled track is followed which takes you quickly away from the not-so-pretty

Gritstone Moor, Kinder Plateau.

The Woolpacks; one of many gritstone rock features on Kinder Scout.

environs of the valley you have just crossed and up over the moor of Chinley Church. Excellent views present themselves towards Greater Manchester to the left, beyond which Winter Hill may be seen. The views right are restricted by the moorland swell, but as the path finally descends, a very inviting prospect of the Kinder Moors is seen, with the narrow thread of the A624 below. The descent now gives glimpses of the next overnight stop, Hayfield, and its field enclosures above. The way down leads via Phoside Farm on a stiled path. Campers can proceed to the attractive site on the River Kinder. 'Comfy-tours' walkers will find a proper roof over their heads in the pleasant town.

The following day sees the Pennine Way joined by a path which goes through, or more properly, round, Tunstead Clough Farm. Two ways present themselves. The longer route goes up to the ancient Edale Cross, around Swineback to Kinder Low and along the western edge of

Higher Shelf Stones from Snake Pass.

the plateau to the Downfall. The shorter way is on a less used track which trends leftwards along subsidiary shoulders below the western edge, to join that path about half a mile from Kinder Downfall.

The Pennine Way has now been joined. The Way has been so well documented that I do not offer any further description. However, the Pennine Way is going to be encountered on many a further sojourn and thus many key points on it will be described where necessary. For now, let's be content to have entered upon the Pennines in perhaps the purest of ways.

Further Walking

Between Hen Cloud and the Kinder Plateau in the environs of the Pennine Way Southern Extension are many walking possibilities. Here are a few suggestions. Hen Cloud, Roaches, Roach End, Gradbach, Allgreave, Danebridge, Gun Hill, Meerbrook Valley return. This is approximately 19km (12 miles).

Kinder Downfall.

A quick ascent of Shutlingsloe from Wildboar Clough, (Clough House). This is 5km (3 miles).

Teggs Nose Country Park, Langley, Ridgegate Reservoir, Macclesfield Forest via Nessit Hill, Shutlingsloe, Wildboarclough, Three Shires Head, Cat & Fiddle, Macclesfield Forest Chapel return. This walk is 22km (13½ miles).

Taxal, Windgather, Cats Tor, Shining Tor, Errwood Reservoir, Goyt Reservoir and Goyt valley return. This is 17km (10½ miles).

The Kinder Plateau offers many wanderings. A classic circuit would go from Edale via Grindslow Knoll, Woolpacks – a superb collection of weathered gritstone rocks – Kinder Low and Downfall, Fairbrook Naize, Seal Edge, Madwoman Stones

and Ringing Roger. This trip is 26km (16 miles), and it truly explores the Plateau's edge.

The Pennine Way next crosses Bleaklow Hill, the approach from Snake Pass, having been much improved underfoot. There is not as much excitement on Bleaklow, but the Wainstones ('the Kiss') catch the eye, and Bleaklow Head seems a very lonely elemental place. A recommended walk in the Bleaklow environs must surely be Alport Bridge, Alport Castles, Howden Reservoir, Derwent Reservoir, with a reversed return journey. The fit ones can go via Alport Castles, Westend Moor, The Ridge, Bleaklow Stones, Bleaklow Head, Doctors Gale, (Pennine Way section), Ladyclough Forest Trail, Cowms Moor and then return. Weather

Wainstones 'The Kiss' Bleaklow Hill.

Descending from Tor Side Clough, Bleaklow to Woodhead Reservoir.

and ground conditions are vital to the safety and enjoyment of walks of this length and nature. The route is about 26km (16miles). Alport Castles represents one of the largest landslips in Britain. Before it occurred there must have been a declivity rivalling or excelling that of Goredale Scar. Even now, the landscape stands proud to the visitor.

Beyond Bleaklow Hill the pylon-inflicted Longdendale houses the overnight possibility of Crowden Youth Hostel. My wife and I could not stay there when walking the Pennine Way from north to south. At our very outset from Kirk Yetholm, surviving Pennine wayfarers gave us horrendous tales of the tummy bug inflicting the southern Pennine youth hostels. The

Snowfall forming graphic patterns on the peat of Black Hill.

Alderman's hill from Dovestone reservoir.

On Standedge.

Standedge Summit.

whole place was a heaving mass of retching walkers, struck down with what seemed to be a respiratory stomach virus. '*Who makes the loo first, wins!*' Crowden and Edale were still closed some two weeks later when we arrived.

There are Peregrine Falcons (and of course at least one wallaby), on the Black Hill massif. I shall not say where the Peregrines are. Observant walkers may well locate the nest site in June. Any entry of this moorland may be accompanied by trepidation through tales of its morass of peat hags. The weather is the essential factor to enjoying Black Hill. I find its environs fascinating despite its reputation. The summit could be used for a scene out of a science fiction film like *Dune*.

However, the hostel at Marsden being closed might persuade the walker to proceed over the fine crags of Laddow Rocks, then divert over Saddleworth Moor to pass Chew Reservoir which is cradled on the lonely moor, then over the western gritstone edge of Saddleworth Moor to observe yet more weathered rock formations and striking vistas over the Dovestones Reservoir. The best way then is over Aldermans Hill heading north to Diggle and over the A62 to stay at Globe Farm on the slopes of Standedge – thus gaining easy and bracing walking the next day over Standedge. (Telephone: 0457 873040 for Globe Farm).

This route avoids the further quagmires of White Moss which are nowhere as scenic as the above route. If possible, visit Black Hill again by walking in *Summer Wine Country*. Go from Digley Reservoir

Northern Rocher (rocks on Standedge).

Peat, Spring and the Northern Rocher Rocks, Standedge.

Towards Greater Manchester from Blackstone Edge.

Halifax seen across the moors from Blackstone Edge.

to point 389 (OS 1:50,000 Number 110) via Wessenden Head to the summit. Return over Woodhead Pass down the A6024 to Yateholm, Riding Wood and Ramsden Reservoirs into Holme and thus back to Digley Reservoir.

Standedge leads to 'The Dinner Stone' and 'Northern Rotcher', utilizing the former Marsden Packhorse Road which is easy going.

There is not much else to shout about on the Pennine Way until you reach Blackstone Edge, though some of us might gawp with disbelief at the tidal flow of traffic beneath our feet on the footbridge over the M62. Blackstone Edge, however, is another great vantage point with some rock architecture to match. The views encompass the wild pennine moors to the south, across to Halifax in

Upper Chelburn Reservoir, Calderbrook and Knowle Moor, from Chelburn Moor.

the east, the Pennine Way ahead over the moor top reservoirs, and to the west and south-west, the environs of Rochdale, the high-rise of greater Manchester, and finally the Western Pennine Moors where Knowle Hill is a prominent lump above Calderbrook.

There is doubt about the authenticity of the Roman roads on Blackstone Edge. They are so well preserved, and thus in reality may be much later, dating from the packhorse period during medieval times. As the eye gets distracted from these relics by the open vistas, it can be jarred by the inherent pylons taking their south Pennine urban links right across these moors. Note, the White House pub sat almost on the pass as a refreshment stop for those pursuing along the Pennine Way. Blackstone Edge and the reservoirs beyond can be easily gained by the motor-ist-cum-walker who parks by the White House, which is situated on the A58.

The juncture is now reached where exploration either side of the spinal Pennine Way is possible. Here, two outstanding walks of several days duration can be made. In fact, it is possible to link them both and make one outing of about a week's duration, but I shall describe them as the separate entities they are.

Chapter 2
THE ROSSENDALE WAY

The main Pennine chain throws out a bulky shoulder to the west, part of which is known as the West Pennine Moors. These lie between Rochdale in the south and Accrington in the north. The Rossendale Way lies entirely inside east Lancashire and roughly follows the borough boundary. It is 72km (45 miles) long, and easy under foot, being mainly over grassy moors. Roads and ribbon development are crossed where necessary. The route meanders in places to take in the best of the terrain and scenery. It can be linked with the Calderdale Way to the east.

Maps   OS 1:50,000 series, Manchester No. 109, and Blackburn, Burnley No. 103. Note that the Rossendale Way is fully described and well mapped in a series of eight leaflets produced by Rossendale Interpretive Project, (these are recommended). Contact Rossendale Borough Council, Town Hall, Rawtenstall, Rossendale, Lancashire BB4 7LZ tel: 0706 217777 or Stubbylee Hall, Bacup, Lancashire, OL130DE. There is also a Tourist Information Centre, 41–5, Kay St Rawtenstall, Lancashire BB4 7LS and a TIC at Hebden Bridge. You start and finish at Bacup.

Transport   Rail Services: the nearest station is Todmorden, British Rail, Halifax, tel: 0422 54207. Bus Services: Transport Enquiry Line, tel: 0772 263333, for all Lancashire bus services. There is also Rossendale Transport, tel: 0706 212337 and Crossville Motor Services, tel: 0244 315400.

Accommodation   Bacup only – there is no accommodation directly on route. TIC, Kay St., Rawtenstall provide an area accommodation list.

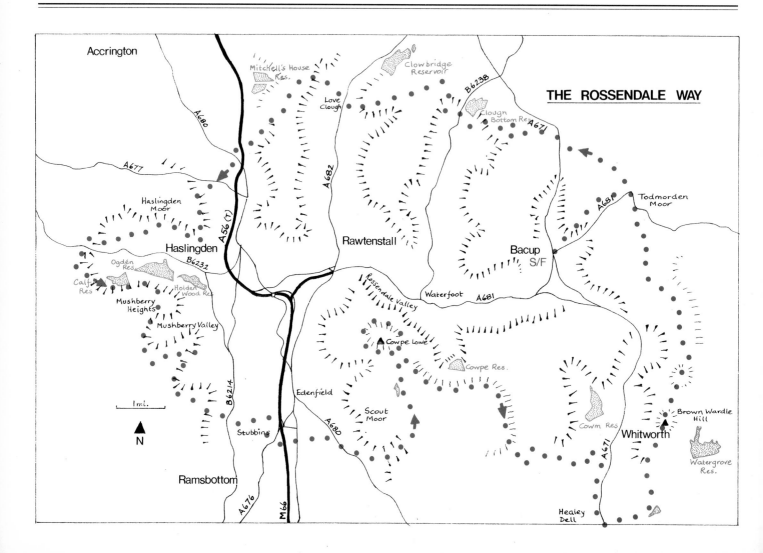

Of all the routes in the Pennines described in this book, the Rossendale Way has proved the most difficult to undertake as an integral outing. There is, to my knowledge, after being inaugurated in 1982, still no accommodation *directly* on this circular walk, except for Bacup. This corner of the Pennines is fan-shaped and although main roads dissect the easy-graded moorland passes, the ribbon development along them appears either domestic, spasmodically retail, or industrial, the last, being bygone relics or still in use.

No one has taken it upon themselves to offer accommodation within several kilometres of any of the strategic points on the Rossendale Way. Therefore, to complete the walk in three days, you have to catch buses from finishing points to the nearest towns. At least the buses are frequent and well noted in the eight leaflets by Rossendale Interpretive Project. Otherwise, it may be possible for a lift to be obtained from a non-walking source, which can be based a few kilometres away at Haslingden, Rawtenstall, Waterfoot or Bacup.

The eight leaflets are well written, very informative and well mapped, but curiously they have not considered the needs of visiting walkers from distant parts. Thus, someone from the Midlands or the south could easily be put off in trying to plan this walk conveniently, and as such might leave it aside for something more attractive. It cannot be said that this is a well-known or fashionable walking area. To the connoisseur of the High Peak or the Yorkshire Dales, Rossendale Borough finds it hard to compete. In fact, in some places, man has made the most ugly intrusions into and on top of the moors. So what is any good about the Rossendale Way?

The Rossendale Way is a walk to do after much of the other Pennines have been explored. It is reminiscent of the Welsh Valleys removed to Lancashire, the exception being the lack of forestry compared to its Welsh counterpart. This journey stimulates deeper thinking, more experienced walkers. It uncovers a living, working, architectural, industrial, historical and ecological environment with some moors as wild as anything in the South Pennines. Although man has tried hard to conquer the nature of these uplands, he

Overlooking Waterfoot and Edgeside in typical Rossendale country.

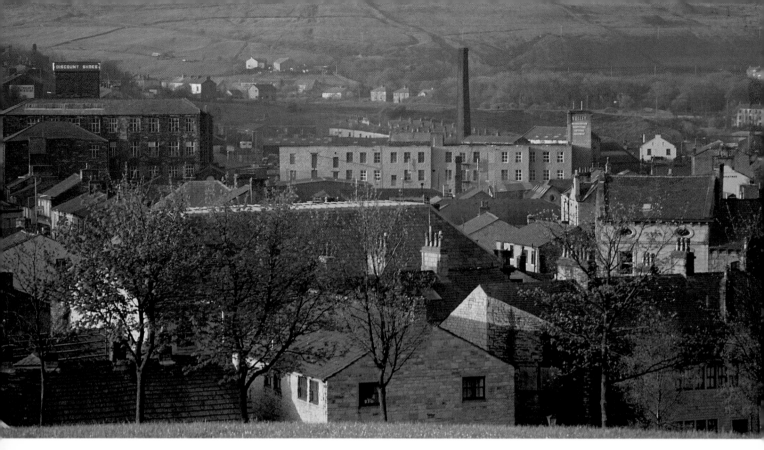

Early morning, Bacup.

has still failed, thus enabling an intricate and often fascinating circuit to be made of these hills. Discerning students of Pennine country will see into its scars, and appreciate its subtle delights, which spring up in a revealing few kilometres. Future Rossen-

dale wayfarers will also get accommodation *en route*, as the Groundwork Project is currently working on this problem.

I will leave the planning of the Rossendale Way to the walker and concentrate on the feel of the walk.

The pleasing feature of good tracks is heartening. The walker does not encounter bogs on the scale of other Pennine areas. For most part, the route uses good bridleways and paths; even old paved tramways to the defunct mines and quarries – a unique feature of these moors.

Out of Bacup, the first feature is a Wesleyan chapel house. Leave the built-up area for a metalled lane which climbs steadily showing off the town cradled in its moorland setting. There are farms and pasture adjacent to this, but an ugly section of pylons mars the skyline at Sharneyford. You come out on the moor by road and an untidy vehicular track left, which is compensated for by good views towards Deerplay and Pendle Hills. Vacate this borough boundary at Heald Top Farm by walking lower, parallel to enclosures, and in all, three farms, at the last one, Height End cross the Burnley–Bacup road. The Old Bacup road is crossed south of the Deerplay Inn, a possible refreshment stop. Green field enclosures in a gently elevated landscape are spoilt by

Thievely Pike and the Deerplay Inn beyond Sharneyford.

the untidy scrap items left around otherwise attractive hill farms dotting the upland. This is an all-too-common feature in this district. However, there are some fine examples of stout gritstone walls near to the descent to Clough Bottom Reservoir, (this involves tricky route-finding). Clough Bottom is an attractive property in a growing surround of young trees.

Reach Lower Cross Farm by road and track. There are good views to Cribden Hill from the route. The track is part of an old highway from Burnley and Clitheroe which winds over a shoulder, and becomes walled; it then finishes at Compston's Cross. Samuel Compston, a local historian and ex-mayor of Rawtenstall erected this monument in 1902, near the site of two ancient crosses. The views are extensive towards Pendle Hill, but you become aware of the impending pylons dwarfing the cross and jarring the landscape. Perhaps the photograph says it all!

Cribden Hill from Windy Bank.

Compston's Cross with impending pylons, this is typical of the South Pennines.

A moorland walk leads past derelict walls giving views over Clowbridge Reservoir, backed by the masts on Hameldon Hill. Views to the south can also be extensive. The descent on Goodshaw Lane is pleasant, being lined with high walls and fine trees, you then reach Loveclough, which is a typical piece of urban ribbon development spreading into the uplands. (**Note**: It is planned to have bunkhouse accommodation in this vicinity.)

There follows a descent through the print works yard to a tricky route-finding exit which climbs steeply to Goodshaw Hill. The next kilometre or so gives elevated walking and makes good progress near dilapidated walls. Look at the fine view west over Accrington and Blackburn, and begin a descent (where the West Pennine Moors are prominent ahead) in order to join a metalled road into Stonefold, an antiquated village where time seems to have stood still. A gap by a barn leads down a road to Lower Stonefold, a tiny hamlet disturbed by the proximity of the updated A56 trunk road. The route eeks out the strip of country adjacent to this highway, then goes underneath it to Rising Bridge. You have suddenly been transported to an urban community, which is not particularly meritorious, so pace through, except perhaps for a stop at the general stores for iron rations or a drink.

There is a decorative style church of St John the Baptist, which is out of context with the 'anywhere' housing. The route then goes by road to reach more attractive rural surrounds. Emerge by the Farmer's Glory, a well-designed public house with a notable datestone. Cross over to a further lane to head towards Copy Farm on open moorland. Bowland and Pendle can be seen behind and Haslingden and the Lower Rossendale Valley can be seen to the left. From Copy Farm, the landscape is more striking, following a moorland scarp edge into the reaches of the Grane Valley, a wild looking area, disturbed only by the Haslingden–Blackburn road. The walk becomes pleasantly attractive as the Calf Hey Reservoir is passed. The climb to the Musbury Quarry has a good view towards Rawtenstall, but the terrain is marred by the spoils. However, this is soon left for the fine crossing of the Musbury Valley, a definite highlight of the Rossendale Way. It sweeps away towards Helmshore

Clowbridge Reservoir and Hameldon Hill from Meadowhead.

Musbury Valley and Tor Hill.

Helmshore from Musbury Valley.

and its prominent church spire, the runnelled watercourses bedecked by shapely trees with the backcloth of Cowpe Lowe Hill across the valley. Close to this, is Tor Hill or Musbury Tor, an attractive promontory. Circle round via Musden Head's ruin to cross this flat-topped hill and turn sharp right to meander over undulating spring lines slowly descending to Stubbins, noting the superb view to the north from the ruins of Goose Pits (Alden Farm), on the way down.

The section from Stubbins provides an ascent into wild country, which is at first civilized, as three major roads are crossed, including the M66, in order to gain height. Inevitably, you will start the dogs barking at the nearby Bleakholt Animal Sanctuary before finding the Bury Old

The Peel Monument on the moor above Ramsbottom, Rossendale.

Road, an ancient highway, and thence the Rochdale Road by the Plane Tree Inn. Curiously, these inns do not provide accommodation! Plod up the road to find steps by a restored farmhouse to reach boggy ground behind 'Lime Leach', a former eighteenth-century loomshop. There is now a good track which gradually skirts the shoulder of Scout Moor. Notice the

Peel monument above Ramsbottom, erected in 1852 in memory of the second Sir Robert Peel. Locate two free-standing gateposts where a track goes left through bracken as the moor closes in. There is a deep gorge on the left, but the route climbs away and up the moor, with a reservoir in the hollow, in country as wild as anywhere in the South Pennines. On

the path is Waugh's Well, a monument utilizing a spring to Edwin Waugh, a Lancashire writer from the nineteenth century.

The whaleback hill of Cowpe Lowe is aimed for and a number of tracks converge including the line of the dismantled tramway. Strangely, the route does not include the summit of Cowpe Lowe, but circumnavigates the hill to reveal superb drops

Approach to Cowpe Lowe in winter conditions.

Moorland, Cowpe Lowe, Rossendale.

north-east towards Waterfoot which is seemingly far below. After almost a complete circuit of the hill you will find a dismantled tramway which leads through quarry spoil heaps. If you divert to a large cairn some metres off route, your eyes will be rewarded by a view over Cowpe Mill and the reservoir, beyond which are rolling Pennine moors. The highest point

Cowpe Mill seen from the Rossendale Way in winter.

in Rossendale, 'Top of the Leach', at 474m (1,555ft) can be visited by a 300-metre detour. It has a viewpointer with distances marked. The Rooley Moor road itself reaches 461m (1,513ft) before descending gradually on a setted section of road which was laid down during the Cotton Famine of the 1860s and is often called the Cotton Famine Road. The blame for the Cotton Famine lies with the Yankees and the Confederates when, during the American Civil War, all supplies of raw cotton from America to Lancashire ceased.

Gaze across the Naden Valley and its three reservoirs, which is dominated from above by Knowle Hill's shapely turret. Pass the cairned Top of Pike and take a left turn at the end of the setted section of road. This eastward section needs to be followed carefully on the map via 'Houses o' th' Hill', on a walled track to Hallfold. Go down through the village and admire the restored stone cottages on the right.

There is a complex exit by a former dyeing mill, a stone bridge and a short incline to find the disused railway line which is then followed through woods to Healey Dell with the River Spodden on the left.

Healey Dell Nature Reserve is an oasis on the edge of Whitworth and Broadley

Healey Dell, a gorge virtually in the suburbs of Rochdale.

An example of a setted road near Top of the Pike.

From Brown Wardle Hill across Whitworth towards Knowle Moor.

which are natural urban extensions of Rochdale. It is a veritable gorge with a mantle of tree cover and the old railway crossing the void on a fine stone viaduct. It is a place to wander round in its own right. Leaflets are obtainable from the tourist information centre at Kay Street Rawtenstall.

Leave the main A671 via Ending Rake to a stone archway into open land. Follow another setted track whose stones were manufactured in Healey Dell to pave Rochdale streets until the mid 1800s. A concrete road and a broken lane go above a reservoir. Curve round Manstone Edge which was the haunt of Byron and is the influence of some of his finest poetry. The flattened dome ahead is Brown Wardle Hill and a moorland path goes directly up its middle to the top. Excellent views over

From Deacon Pasture over Ramsden Clough Reservoir towards Stoodley Pike and Calderdale.

Watergrove Reservoir lead the eye to Hollingworth Lake and Blackstone Edge, whilst opposite, Knowle Hill peeps over the intervening hillsides above Whitworth. From the trig point a descent follows, then a climb up Middle Hill and Hades Hill, a dreadful crossing totally defaced by scrap iron machinery, vehicles and open quarrying. No wonder it is called 'Hades'! However, better is to come, because a mere few hundred metres beyond Hades the walk resumes a fine moorland flavour. There is a very pretty view over Deacon Pasture to Ramsden Clough Reservoir, beyond which Calderdale and its surrounding hills are well illustrated, with, notably on the right, Stoodley Pike's monument which sits on the moor edge. There are also some fine panoramas off to the left, of Shawforth and Trough Gate which occupies a shallow valley leading into Bacup. The walk continues on easy elevated grassy moorland, but with the constant reminder of man's dwellings and other architectural implements dotted regularly over the landscape. This moor continues to the A681 road to complete the circuit at Sharneyford. It only remains to use the original path in reverse to descend to Bacup.

Chapter 3
THE CALDERDALE WAY

Maps	OS 1:50,000 series Nos. 103 and 104. 1:25,000 series of the 'South Pennines'. The Pathfinder series sheet SE 02/12, 1:25,000 series which I recommend! An 80-km (50-mile) circular walk, linking eight independent communities, that were drawn together in 1974 to form the Metropolitan Borough of Calderdale, West Yorkshire. A walk which is most attractive where mill towns merge into moorland hills.
	Note: There is a comprehensive guide booklet, 'The Calderdale Way', published by Calderdale MBC, available for a small sum from Tourist Information Centres at 1, Bridgegate, Hebdon Bridge, and Piece Hall, Halifax, HX7 8JP, tel: 0422 68725.
Transport	Rail Services: British Rail, Halifax, tel: 0422 54207 for free summaries of trains through the Calder Valley.
	Bus Services: Ask Tourist Information for details in the form of the leaflet 'Walk Calderdale Way by Bus', or otherwise Metro or West Yorks PTE, Metro House, West Parade, Wakefield WF1 1JS.
Accommodation	There is a good choice of accommodation on or near the route. Ask the TIC for the free booklet 'Where to Stay in Calderdale'. I recommend night 1 at Mankinholes Youth Hostel, night 2 at Heptonstall, night 3 at the Duke of York Inn Stone Chair, Shelf.
	You start and finish at Clay House, West Vale.
	Day 1 Clay House to Mankinholes 19km (12 miles): Day 2 Mankinholes to Heptonstall 18km (11½ miles): Day 3 Heptonstall to Stone Chair 23km (14½ miles): Day 4 Stone Chair to Clay House 19km (12 miles).

THE CALDERDALE WAY

Calderdale is a living Pennine environment, having innumerable places of great interest within the perimeters of the Calderdale Way. It is a crime not to extend your stay or revisit this area. Much about the locality is found in the Tourist Information Centre at Piece Hall, Halifax, a unique grandiose building of significant architectural and historical interest, which is most deserving of special mention.

The Piece Hall

This marvellous building is a one-off monument to the great days of cloth manufacture. The name refers to the lengths of cloth, (pieces), sold at 30 yards long. An old cloth hall in Halifax became unable to cope with the demands of trade. The Piece Hall was planned in 1774 and opened in 1779. Thirty-five years of brisk business saw changes in textile industry mechanization, leading to the building of many mills. Weavers became redundant as merchants only needed to visit two or three mills in the locality for purchases. Piece Hall trade slackened such that in 1871 it was converted into a wholesale fish, fruit and vegetable market. It became the venue for public events. In 1928 it was scheduled an ancient monument and several philanthropic ideas were floated about its future use. No satisfactory solution was found and various schemes were shelved. Somehow, the weird and wonderful minds of 1960s planners whose environmental wonders we often curse today, nearly got the place demolished! It was saved by just one council vote!

Today, thankfully sees the Piece Hall fully restored and in daily use. It was reopened in 1976 showing off John Hope's original architectural design which is Classically Roman, with massive rustic piers supporting semi-circular arches on the ground floor or the Arcade Level, square jointed columns on the Rustic Level, and a continuous gallery of round doric columns on the top floor or the Colonnade. Each corner supports an internal staircase and there are three entrances on the north,

Piece Hall, Halifax.

south and west sides. It is now a grade 1 listed building with a mixture of museums, markets and shops surrounding a courtyard of 10,000 square yards.

This book is primarily about wild rural landscape. However, I love the buildings of Calderdale, and the Piece Hall is an inspiring place.

The Calderdale Way

The Calderdale Way was officially opened in 1978. It weaves an intricate and subtle route, finding the most attractive way to encircle the Calder Valley without getting swallowed up in large areas of population. It is predominantly a gritstone landscape of heathery moorland, surviving the encroachment of man's dwellings and industrial places which are found clustered along valley floors and more scattered on to moorsides. Nowhere else in England is the landscape so saturated with footpaths, as they link the rural and urban communities. Many are old packhorse routes and are paved with flagstones or 'causeys' some of which are encountered on the Way. Full marks to the Calderdale Way Association who planned it.

Day 1

Clay House Visitor Centre may see your car languish for the next four days while your feet do the miles. It is a fine three-gabled seventeenth-century house with displays and booklets about Calderdale.

The route starts innocuously, passing a builder's yard but soon establishes itself above the upper fringe of Northdean Wood. One or two good views briefly open up over Elland before the eye notes the lower Calder Valley and the cooling towers by Elland Park Wood. The Wainhouse Tower, looking like some minaret and the fringes of Halifax can be seen across the valley which supports a fine rail viaduct beyond Copley. Norland Moor, a gritstone plateau, opens up views of

Turgate Delph on Norland Moor, towards Sowerby.

Ripponden.

almost two-thirds the area to be covered. It tries to become a gritstone edge by Turgate Delph. Grasses and heather, however, predominate. Ahead, the hillside village of Mill Bank is framed by Crow Hill.

Returning to farmed areas, the numerous pastures on the lower level lead to a drop into Ripponden with its steepled church and Pennine Farm museum. This houses a rush cart. The ancient ceremony of a rush-bearing procession is held between Luddenden, Sowerby and Ripponden on the first weekend in September. It makes a fascinating spectacle, terminating on the Sunday at St Bartholomew's Church in Rippenden.

The route goes from here via the packhorse bridge over the River Ryburn. Then you cross the main road and ascend Royd

Mill Bank – an attractive hillside village near Ripponden.

hilltop location, actually belies the circuitous and undulating walk required to reach it.

Note the Methodist Chapel in Mankinholes, before leaving through the attractive field enclosures for Lumbutts and beyond. The black uncleaned spire of Todmorden's Unitarian Church is passed before entering into the far end of town, a dingy place, with the sudden encroachment of heavy traffic. Perhaps Todmorden's best feature is the fine upstanding (and cleaned) classical façade of its town hall, but you would have to make a diversion into the centre to admire it before retracing your steps. The stiff climb out of Todmorden on the route proper, up a wooded lane, gives excellent views over the town, now looking much nicer in its cloak of woodland.

Dobroyd Castle is a Victorian 'Tudor' building set in its own pastures around which the route passes. After crossing the brow of the hill, a fine, squat whitewashed 'weavers' cottage, now Todmorden Edge Farm, is encountered, beyond which a superb bird's-eye overlook of Centre Vale

Causey Stones above Cragg Vale.

Lane. The name 'Royd' as in 'Mytholmroyd' means a clearing of land and is common in the Calderdale environs. A fine view of Mill Bank can be seen from High Field near Soyland. It is a pleasurable village straddled across the contour of the hillside. West of Mill Bank you can glance in retrospect at sweeping moorland vistas. Hereabouts the gritstone walls and a gloomy ruin are, as in parts of West Yorkshire and East Lancashire, somewhat bedraggled.

The feeling brightens when Stoodley Pike's Crimea monument catches the eye across the gap of Cragg Vale, which is descended to, via the first encounter with a fine causey stone pathway.

The towered church of 'St John the Baptist in the Wilderness', nestles in the serenely wooded Cragg Vale. The road then makes for uphill walking to Withens Clough Reservoir, beyond which a true moorland waste leads to the '*Ti Deum Stone*', a sacred spot where coffins were rested, on an old packhorse trail. Ahead now, are wide expanses of Upper Calderdale which stretch away as the descent is made on causey stones to Mankinholes and the Youth Hostel. Stoodley Pike on the brow of the moor is always likely to rivet the gaze.

Day 2

The fact that Heptonstall appears a short distance across the valley, perched on its

is glimpsed with its park and bowling greens. Descend to this via the beeches of Buckley Wood, again crossing a main highway. Another stiff slog circles round reaching Whirlaw Common and giving yet another angle on Todmorden. The Great Bridestones, (some of which became pregnant before the wedding) are worth a diversion up to 437m (1,435ft). In particular, note the 'Bottlestone', a large weird and well-undercut gritstone rock whose very slim base defiantly supports its weight. Return to the causey stones on Whirlaw Common and follow the Way as it contours the moor to reach Great Rock, a graffiti-ridden gritstone tor. What a shame there are human elements who have to deface nature! After this, a green lane, moor and farms lead to Blackshaw Head, a

Morning mists at Lumbutts and Stoodley Pike.

Todmorden from the Calderdale Way.

Centre Vale view from Todmorden Edge.

Weavers' Cottage, Todmorden Edge.   *Great Bridestones, Bridestones Moor, Todmorden.*

Heptonstall from near Pecket Well.

bleak looking settlement. A scattered ribbon development is seen as the eye comes to rest on the tower of Heptonstall Church.

Long Row Bottom is a peaceful spot shared with the Pennine Way. A stone clapper bridge at Hebble Hole spans the brook of Golden Water. Cross this bridge to get to further causey stones and follow a pleasant system of field paths above the woods and tree tops. You will be aware of the ever-impending gorge below, particu-

larly on reaching Heptonstall Quarry which gives a superb view over Mytholm. Heptonstall, a classic English hilltop village, whose many features of interest are described in history trails produced by the Calder Civic Trust (ask at the Tourist Information Centre, Piece Hall for details). Heptonstall is a place to linger, and it does not take too much time to have a look around, and it is wise to seek accommodation here. Staying at Heptonstall enables you to take a look at the

grammar school, the ruins of the old church, the graveyard with stones and slabs juxtaposed to the newer, yet worthy Victorian building. The Methodist Chapel is probably the oldest of its type still in use and the famous John Wesley preached there.

Day 3

Today sees a fairly strenuous walk involving several ups and downs over varied

Heptonstall – the Victorian ('new') church seen from the old ruin.

Moor, but keeping always above the many field enclosures. Nearby at Old Town is Acre Mills, now a vintage car museum known as 'Automobilia'. On the moor a short distance later, a stone pillar stands isolated, almost forlorn. This is 'Churn Milk Joan'. It is of dubious origin but it could be a medieval cross or boundary stone. The legendary Joan was a milk maid who lost her way and died out on the moor.

You swing left and north, descending towards Luddenden Dean. Next, Jerusalem Farm campsite is passed, hugging the lowest slopes of the attractive wooded dean (or valley), before another climb finds you at Saltonstall, a cluster of weavers' cottages in a grid of dark drystone walls. Further up, there are excellent retrospective views of Luddenden Dean. Then, near Hunter Hill, the white spec on the moorland skyline is Withins Inn, the highest pub in West Yorkshire. Behind you, excellent moorland vistas stretch back towards Stoodley Pike, now a mere speck. There is a chance to imbibe on reaching the Sportsman Inn on the A629 Keighley Road. Here the Way passes through richer farming country as it cleverly avoids Illingworth's regimented housing estates. Holdsworth House Farm, dated 1642, is the fine residential property

scenery. Gravity is with you at the start, via a steep track aside the Methodist Chapel leading down across the road and thence steeply into Hebden Dale. Views from near the road crossing, below to Hebden Dale and Hebden Bridge are quite spectacular and the clusters of many storeyed buildings hugging the steep hillsides of Hebden Dale give an impression that this is some model town creation. Woodland conceals the route, which having reached the dale almost immediately strikes up steeply to Pecket Well, where the Pecket War memorial (a miniature Stoodley Pike construction), is compared when heads are turned, to its more grandiose sister on the moor behind Heptonstall which is seen to fine advantage.

There follows a bracing few kilometres contouring the southern edge of Midgley

Farms and field patterns, Midgley Moor.

Saltonstall, a collection of eighteenth-century Weavers' Cottages.

The reservoir at Moor Bottom with the Withens Inn over 400m (1,300ft) on the skyline.

typifying the architecture of hill cottages and farms in Calderdale.

From the crest on which Catherine Slack lies comes another drop into a valley whose beauty belies its position. Between the urban sprawls of Halifax and Bradford, Shibden Valley threads a little haven of rural delicacy, an oasis of peace and quiet seemingly cut off from traffic and other disturbances. It makes a fine crossing from side to side, noting on the way down, the seventeenth-century Scout Hall in a sylvan setting, sadly now abandoned. Shibden Hall, outside Halifax is a must on the itinerary of any period building enthusiast, (details from the TIC at Piece Hall, Halifax). At or near Adders Gate Farm, which is gained by a haul up the side of Shibden Valley, there is a good view along the dale. The next intrusion of buildings is

Carpet Mill at Bailiff Bridge, near Brighouse.

the village of Stone Chair. Although only 23km (14½miles) have been walked, this day surely must finish at the Duke of York Inn. It is a very well appointed hostelry, so why move on? Better to taste its food and comfortable accommodation.

Day 4

The creature comforts of the Duke of York are left, but not before observing the actual stone chair protruding from the pavement opposite. It was a flat seat erected in 1737 for those awaiting the horse-drawn transport. It was re-erected in 1891. From the backs of terraced houses, the A6036 Bradford to Halifax road is crossed into Shelf Hall Park. This green interlude continues into woods where a stream is crossed by a small waterfall. The woodland fringe is a pleasant walk until Norwood Green village is entered. This too seems a highly desirable living place where houses mingle with patches of village green.

For some distance the route traverses strips of semi-rural country encountering carpet mills, in particular the proud factory of Firths Carpets at Bailiff Bridge, connected in two parts by an arch spanning the road. A steady climb now ensues, reaching eighteenth-century Woolrow Farm. There are views of the Iron Age Castle Hill and Emley Moor television mast. Downhill once again will give views of Brighouse, a busy market town intruding on the rurality of the journey. On the other side of the coin, there is opportunity for refreshment in Brighouse, maybe some tasty West Yorkshire fish and chips. (All over the Pennines, there are great fish and chip shops mainly using old fashioned dripping in which to fry. All I can say is, this Brummie thinks they are a cut above anything in his own city, so any fish and chip shop owners from the Midlands reading this, take note!)

The Calderdale Way passes along the streets of Brighouse from the Canal Basin with its attendant boats. The canal system of the mid-eighteenth century enabled

Brighouse Canal Basin.

goods to be brought from the coast via Goole and Wakefield. It is canal walking that occupies the next couple of kilometres. Observe Ganney Lock as the watercourse is crossed by a bridge. The industrial nature of the landscape is now swapped for an excursion into Freemans Wood. As if for the exercise, this diversion is quitted by a 240-step descent to a farm, Fort Montague at Cromwell Bottom. Again, it is uphill into Cromwell Wood, before peaking against the outskirts of Southowram. Some road walking gives vistas towards Sowerby Crow Hill, Wainhouse Tower and parts of Halifax. Seeing Norland Moor tells of a soon-to-be-completed circuit. Prior to completion, however, the Elland bypass must be crossed – if you dare – in order to reach a canal at Longlees Lock. The canal is traversed on a railed walkway turning right towards Salterhebble to join the Stainland Road (A6026), near an underpass.

The Salterhebble Canal Basin was restored in 1986/7, having been abandoned from use in 1942. It is well worth a visit. All that now remains is a short walk back to Clay House, completing a detailed journey that encapsulates all the facets of West Yorkshire.

Chapter 4

THE BRONTË ROUND

A very interesting 37-km (23-mile) circuit of the Brontë moors was devised by Derek Magnall of Tottington near Bury. He provides a step by step description in a leaflet, acts as a recorder of the route's passengers, and provides certificates and badges for those so recorded for a small remittance. Ideally, the walk can be done in two stages with an overnight in Haworth, although strong walkers could achieve it within a day. The interest lies in the history and natural land form, which in part is quite unique to the Pennines.

Maps	OS 1:25,000 leisure series the 'South Pennines'.
Transport	Rail Services: British Rail Keighley, Todmorden. Also note Worth Valley Railway, from Keighley to Oxenhope.
	Bus Services: tel: 0274 732237, or Metro or West Yorks PTE, Metro House, West Parade, Wakefield WF1 1JS.
Accommodation	Haworth Youth Hostel tel: 0535 42234 or Mankinholes Youth Hostel, tel: 0706 812340. Otherwise, you can get 'Where to Stay in West Yorkshire' from the TIC, Hebden Bridge, or Piece Hall, Halifax.
	You start and finish at the car park Bridgegate, Hebden Bridge.

Hebden Bridge is a one-off town. It lies on the junction of the River Calder and its tributary Hebden Water, the latter, having carved a very deep gorge which penetrates well into the moors. All valley sides are steep, and the buildings of Hebden Bridge were built to hug these steep contours, such that they are often multi-storeyed with entrances on significantly different levels from front to back. Their curves and lines with occasional chimney stacks make a unique setting, especially when viewed from the road to Hepton-stall. It is a definite tourist attraction and has a profusion of antique and art-orientated shops. It is almost on a grid pattern centrally with a park and land-scaped canalside to complete the scene.

The walk goes north out of town and needs to be followed carefully to the west side of the river first by Pack Horse Bridge, then by the cricket club and bowling club on the left. Keep to the wide track in order to aim for the crossing of Hebden Water at Midgeholes via a bridge. Another wide track leads through the glades of Foul Scout Wood with Hebden Water down below. The gorge bends round to the right near to the river level once again, then climbs to the base of Hardcastle Crags. There are large hummocks in the

valley caused by a landslip supposedly over a thousand years or more ago. It is possible to climb them and proceed along a ridge which winds for a few hundred metres before regaining your route. At a point where the stream of Rowshaw Clough tumbles down to Hebden Water, go right and up along its side on a path lined with rhododendrons which climbs the valley side to Walshaw, where during the 1860s much rebuilding of the old farm houses took place. Walshaw was a former cleated farm settlement with open field systems.

Bluebells in Foul Scout Wood.

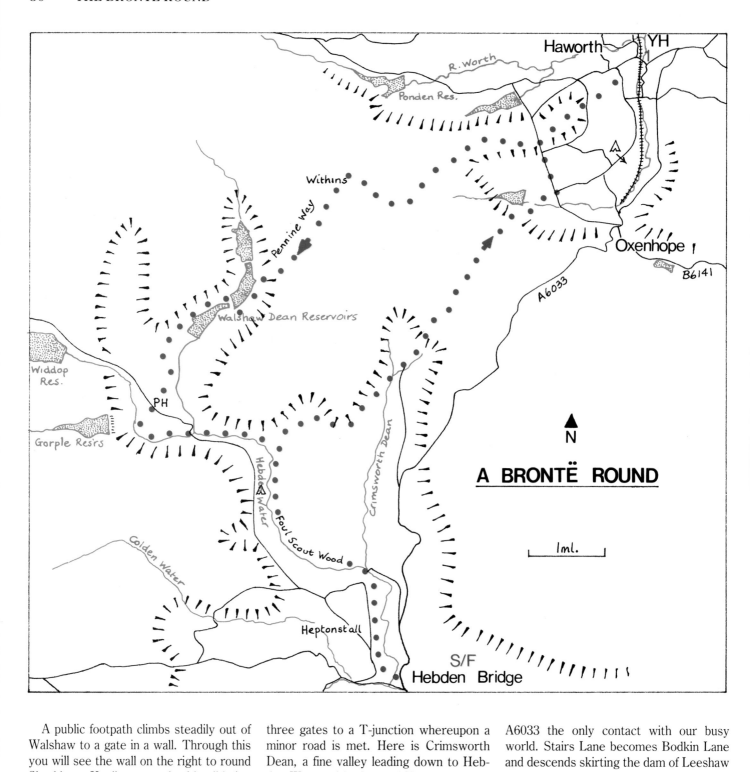

A BRONTË ROUND

N

1 ml.

A public footpath climbs steadily out of Walshaw to a gate in a wall. Through this you will see the wall on the right to round Shackleton Knoll – a moorland knoll being exactly what it is. Soon, a ruined farm, typical of many such abandoned dwellings in this district, marks the way on a wide track which goes left before passing through three gates to a T-junction whereupon a minor road is met. Here is Crimsworth Dean, a fine valley leading down to Hebden Water with views of Heptonstall and Stoodley Pike. Go up Stairs Lane, which degenerates into a wide track along to Top of Stairs, at 426m (1,398ft), well out on the moors with the tiny vehicles along the A6033 the only contact with our busy world. Stairs Lane becomes Bodkin Lane and descends skirting the dam of Leeshaw Reservoir, to become Lee Lane as it threads through the collection of buildings which comprise Moorside. Here, Moorside lane to the left is taken to a car park on Penistone Hill with toilets for the

Crimsworth Dean southwards to Heptonstall and Stoodley Pike.

Bodkin Lane, Bodkin Farm and Leeshaw Reservoir.

needy! Penistone Country Park is the reclamation of quarry spoils which overlook the Worth Valley. It may be handy for locals to wander, but there is too much left of its former use and as such I do not find it attractive. From here, pace down into Haworth if staying the night, although the walk officially begins its turnaround here. Going to Haworth enables the historically and literary minded of us to study the lives of Britain's most famous literary family, the Brontës, by visiting the Brontë Parsonage Museum. Except for their father, who outlived all his family, the Brontës did not get far in the longevity stakes! Two daughters died at ten and eleven, respectively, whilst Ann only reached twenty-eight, Emily thirty, and Charlotte, who having only recently married, much

Haworth main street with attendant tourists.

against her father's wishes, died whilst carrying her first child at thirty-nine. It is interesting to note that Branwell, their brother, who failed in his genuine efforts to become a portrait artist, visited the local apothecary which is still in the village, to obtain opium. By carefully reading a sign to this effect on the doorway of the building, note how the word 'indirect' has been painted over with the word 'direct' referring to the opium as a cause of his death. Is this to lessen the shame, I ask? Although the Brontë sisters did receive some success whilst alive, it was nothing to the sudden national and international acclaim that was bestowed upon them long after their deaths. So, tell everyone else to buy this book now, whilst I live!

The return route follows the Top Withins signs and overlooks enclosures before descending to Lower Laithe Reservoir with heath and moor on the left. Aim for Brontë Falls and Brontë Bridge, compelling really only in their name, although they are situated in an attractive dell formed by South Dean and Sladen Beck – two names for a single watercourse. The bridge is small, but arches gently over the beck, which you move uphill from to curve round Harbour Hill. Ahead is the isolated, ruinous and quite forlorn Top Withins.

Whether or not Withins was actually Emily Brontë's *Wuthering Heights*, hardly matters today, for popular opinion has related it firmly to her novel. Its structure was obviously proud in its day and it occupies a position well above all the other one-time moorland dwellings in this vicinity. The occupiers must have been brave to live here on an exposed heather and peat moor, where inclement weather would have been the norm and there were probably some very hard winters. Arriving there in a moorland mist would aliken it to a ghost story rather than Emily Brontë's novel, though even that was austere in character. The Brontë Society placed a plaque there fixed to a wall, stating the building does not fit the description she made of *Wuthering*

Top Withins, the 'Wuthering Heights' of the Brontë novel.

Walshaw Dean Reservoir with Widdop Reservoir beyond.

Heights, but that the high moorland setting is typical of its supposed location.

The moorland is rough, often wet especially when going across peaty grass in order to utilize the Pennine Way in north to south mode. Views of Stoodley Pike and Blackstone Edge open up, and the observant might notice underfoot a number of bench marks on the path which leads to the two Walshaw Dean Reservoirs. Cross between the two lakes on a grass strip. Pick up the reservoir road for 2 kilometres then bear left on a track for 50 metres and go through a wooden gate which is fenced in, to cross enclosures to the only building of consequence in site, The Pack Horse Inn on the Hebden Bridge–Colne road. 'Go back and miss a turn', all those who resist stopping at this seventeenth-century inn for liquid refreshment.

The Pack Horse Inn, Widdop, a seventeenth-century hostelry.

Hebden Water, a beautiful wooded gorge.

Take the road to the Pennine Way some 400 metres away. Follow Graining Water, leaving the Pennine Way to swing round to Blake Dean. The road snakes to a bridge and a good track left leads over a footbridge on the stream in a fine declivity. Follow the path which runs right by Hebden Water and begins to cut a very picturesque valley that soon becomes wooded.

This joins the original Pennine Way route to Walshaw. Better still, follow the very edge of Hebden Water for at least 5km (3 miles), crossing the river by footbridges, until reaching Midge Holes. This is a very attractive route as it goes through beautiful wooded gorge scenery. From Midge Holes, all that remains is to retrace the original route back to Hebden Bridge.

Further Walking

There is a huge variety of walks around Hebden Bridge. Consult the tourist information centre at Hebden Bridge, regarding the booklet 'Pennine Walks Around Hebden Bridge' that is published by Calder Civic Trust.

Chapter 5
THE PENDLE WAY

This 72km (45-mile) circuit covers the perimeter of the borough of Pendle in north-east Lancashire. The walk takes in the western edge of the main Pennine chain, including the optional ascent of Boulsworth Hill (or Lad Law). It reaches far across a sweeping populated valley that houses the well-known Lancashire towns of Nelson and Colne, above which rises the dominant Pendle Hill, at 557m (1,827ft). It is a landmark that is observed from many parts of the walk, and although separated from the main Pennine chain, it has an isolated position and a bulk to render it Pennine in character. You will encounter a variety of environments, from farmland pasture, to canals, rivers and heathery moorland. However, there are no extensive woods in these surrounds. The Pendle Way is surely the best waymarked walk in the Pennines.

Maps	OS 1:50,000 No. 103, Blackburn, Burnley.
	A series of eight leaflets very well described and mapped is available at a small charge from the TIC, Nelson, tel: 0282 692890, they are also available at the Information Centre, Barley Picnic Site, tel: 601893. The TIC at Hebden Bridge has been known to stock these leaflets also.
Transport	Rail Services: the nearest station is Colne, (this is only manned part-time), so tel: 0282 25421. From north or south, you change at Preston.
	Bus Services: for details of all bus services phone Lancashire County Information Centre, Broadway, Nelson, Lancashire BB9 9SJ, tel: 0282 698533. Also Burnley and Pendle Transport Company, tel: 0282 25244/5.
Accommodation	You can get details from the TIC at Nelson, (see above). I personally recommend Mrs Robinson, Monks House, 5, Manchester Road, Barnoldswick, tel: 0282 814423. I also highly recommend Mrs P Hodgson, Parson Lee Farm, Wycoller, Lancashire, tel: 0282 864747. This is an eighteenth-century farmhouse in a splendid location right on the Pendle Way. Your host is willing to drive Pendle wayfarers to and from starting and finishing points each day, thus enabling them to travel lighter and stay only at one location where cars are safely parked.

The official start of the walk is at Barrowford at The Pendle Heritage Centre. There are several possibilities for a start and finish at various locations. We started from Barley, a pretty village sheltered under the east scarp of Pendle Hill. It has fine stone cottages, a pub and restaurant and an information centre/picnic site. It is a natural base for the ascent of Pendle Hill if tackled separately.

A stream (Pendle Water), is followed on a good trail, with conifer groves on the opposite bank. A farm is threaded into a larch wood, (one of few woods of any consequence on the route). This leads pleasantly to open green farm pastures in undulating country which meets again with Pendle Water, that can be crossed by a series of stepping stones. A climb gives good retrospective views of Roughlee village and Pendle Hill, though try to ignore the metal boxes of the Pendle Caravan Park, dotted regimentally across the lower valley, a definite intrusion on a

Stepping stones, Pendle Water, Roughlee.

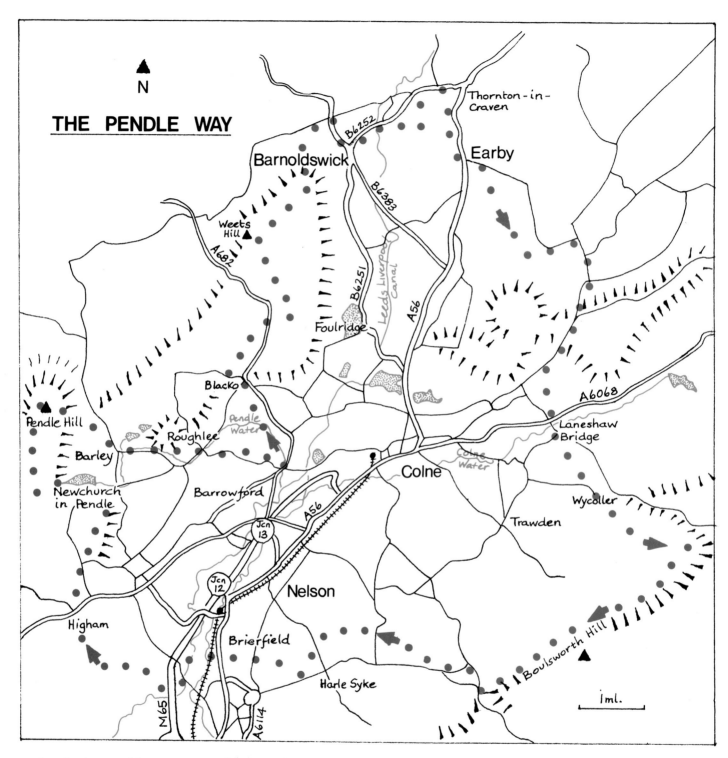

↑
N

THE PENDLE WAY

Thornton-in-Craven

Barnoldswick

Earby

B6252

B6383

Weets Hill

A682

B6251

Leeds Liverpool Canal

A56

Foulridge

Blacko

Pendle Water

A6068

Pendle Hill

Roughlee

Laneshaw Bridge

Barley

Colne Water

Colne

Newchurch in Pendle

Barrowford

A56

Wycoller

Trawden

Jcn 13

Nelson

Jcn 12

Higham

Boulsworth Hill

Brierfield

Harle Syke

1 ml.

M65

A6114

verdant landscape. More pastures with glimpses of Nelson and Colne lead down to Barrowford via a final lane. The main road is crossed into the grounds containing Pendle Heritage Centre which holds exhibitions on farming, local history, architecture and the Pendle Witches. Outside are a walled garden and a fourteenth-century cruck barn. The river path meets the main road where a right and a left turn are made, noting a fine packhorse bridge over the watercourse.

From hereon there follows a steady ascent, almost imperceptible at first, tracking Blacko Water upstream to Water-

Pendle Hill above Nelson.

Blacko Tower from The Old Guisburn Road.

meetings, where it is joined by Pendle Water. First climb, then level out to walk in pasture to Blacko Foot Farm. Join Blacko Water again, but leave it soon to go right following Admergill Water in a quiet gentle dale away from any disturbance. Admergill Hall is a seventeenth-century house with period mullion windows. Stansfield or Blacko Tower has been glimpsed several times on the way and now it lies on top of the right hand valley side. Jonathan Stansfield, a grocer and landowner built this folly about 1890 to try to see into Ribblesdale from the top of the tower. That view was impossible from here. He should have built it on the higher, bleaker, Weets Hill. To get there, the pretty dale is ascended right to cross the main Guisburn Road and uphill beyond

Weets Hill with Barnoldswick below and Yorkshire Dales country beyond.

where a good stone wall is followed on a green path until it reaches the Guisburn Old Road. Go up this to an isolated dwelling. From here, enter moorland and traverse Weets Hill which is a fine crossing, giving great views over Ribblesdale, beyond which lie Bowland's moors, Ingleborough and the Yorkshire Dales. Attermire Scar is the notched skyline nearer and right of Ingleborough. Great Whernside can be seen on the far horizon whilst right, note the Aire Gap, Pinhaw Beacon and the Bronte Moors with the nearer Boulsworth Hill a dominant whaleback. As the descent is made, a great overlook of Barnoldswick appears. This former Yorkshire town is headed for in a lengthy

descent, with the above views holding the gaze most of the way down.

To take in the best of Barnoldswick's surrounds, a circuitous way around the perimeter of the town is made. Bancroft Mill was the last cotton weaving shed to be built in Barnoldswick in 1922. It survives today as an intact engine house, open to the public. A semi-rural walk leads down to the Leeds and Liverpool Canal which is followed easily for a couple of kilometres passing mills that had an easy access to a water supply and transport. The canal wiggles round to Greenberfield Locks, an attractive setting with a little kiosk where information on the canal can be obtained. The canal is raised from

surrounding country which has taken on a significant green colour with drumlins forming small swelling hills in this brief flirtation into limestone country. Exit the canal and walk across the main road reaching St Mary Le Gill Church, situated actually above a small gill and is seemingly isolated from the populace but is quite near a Rolls Royce factory! A climb and descent lead to the road again, where you should note the church opposite at Thornton-in-Craven. Pastures now lead to Earby. A road goes past Earby Mines Museum via terraces. This museum has a notable drive wheel in the grounds. This road then passes by factories and a strip of urban development which takes on a village character to pass the youth hostel and go into farming country.

There follows a protracted section of farmland, which in my view is capable of being anywhere, thus rather character-less, and perhaps the most monotonous piece of walking on the Pendle Way. Eventually the route enters a valley and penetrates into hill country which gives intimations of the better scenery to come.

Greenberfield Locks, Leeds–Liverpool Canal.

Enter a clough via Harden Clough Farm, with a bracken hillside left and a copse to the right. Climb up this into the hills and cap a crest which suddenly opens up wide-ranging views south, east and west. The road at Black Lane Ends was the first turnpike in Pendle built in 1755 from Colne to Skipton. Only the Hare and Hounds pub retains its original guise in this remote settlement. Thank goodness it does, for a

Earby Mines museum.

pint and platter are the answer to flagging limbs at this distance.

Beyond the pub, panoramas stretch towards Boulsworth Hill, Pendle Hill, Laneshaw Bridge and Trawden. The general downward trend, though undulat-ing, is a welcome prospect. First, however, walk the lane and then turn right to go up the easy Knarrs Hill which is another fine viewpoint. From here, a long descent over high pastures leads down to a stream in a shallow valley. This is gene-rally tracked into Laneshaw Bridge, a village set on the crossroads for a number of turnpike roads of bygone times. (Now, we just pay road tax!)

The walk from Laneshaw Bridge takes on an increasingly attractive riverside path. Watercourses always seem to take any boredom out of a lengthy plod. If nothing else, there is the tranquillizing effect of the rippling, flowing water. You can sense that this path is leading some-where more intriguing, and it does. Thus, you enter Wycoller village and the country park, first passing seventeenth-century Lane Ends Farm. Wycoller is a pre-Industrial Revolution hamlet that relied on farming and weaving. The Industrial Revolution was responsible for an exodus to the new mills. Much later, the village was purchased by the Water Board, and it became deserted, with plans for a reser-voir to flood the valley. This did not come to pass, the Friends of Wycoller being formed around the 1940s, highlighting the

Wycoller and the Pack Horse Bridge.

hamlet's merits, particularly Wycoller Hall, the packhorse and clapper bridges. Wycoller Hall is reputedly Ferndean Manor in Charlotte Brontë's famous novel *Jane Eyre*.

Follow the tree-lined beck and pass a wooden bridge. This wooden bridge repla-ced an Iron Age single stone bridge. Hav-ing been there for centuries, it was broken up into three pieces by a great flash flood in May 1989 which also did damage to Wycoller Visitor Centre, dwellings and cars.

Just a short distance up the unmetalled lane is Parson Lee Farm. It has only had four family owners since its construction in 1736. It is a working farm and a guest house occupied by the Hodgsons who, besides showing you a pictorial record of the flash flood will readily tell you comical but true tales of the characters and com-

who owned Wycoller Hall. Some say he died (along with the horse) doing the jump on horseback! Others say he did it on foot and managed to clear the deadly gap.

The Pendle Way pulls away from the farm for several hundred metres to veer right on to a moorland track, crossing a beck in a hollow to emerge on the other side where you can use causey stones for a short distance. Strong walkers are recommended to divert off route at Spoutley Lumb to ascend, with the help of guideposts, the side of Boulsworth Hill. This is a fine sentinel on the edge of the main Pennine chain, forming the western end to a vast moor, which if studied on the map stretches a full 26km (16 miles) to the east only to end near Halifax. From the summit it is possible to see Heptonstall, Stoodley Pike, Great Bridestones, and in the other arc, Pendle Hill and the hills of the Yorkshire Dales. The view will have to be possible, otherwise you will question the effort exerted, as you join the original route just before it climbs a pass at 314m (1,029ft). This descends to the Coldwell Reservoirs and is sheltered by imposing gritstone walls. (Note that the Boulsworth Hill paths are concessionary on Water Board land and are not marked on maps, though well marked by posts.)

Wycoller Beck towards Boulsworth Hill.

The Way goes by Catlow Brook but is deceptive in that it undulates and does not follow directly by the stream. The exit from Catlow Bottoms is tedious by diverting uphill then through a quarry. The tricky passage through Southfield Fold reveals a fine prospect of Pendle Hill above the rows of terraces in Nelson with a steepled church a focal point in the town. Having descended to a reservoir, unfortunately another hill has to be climbed to Briercliffe. This is located on a road to Nelson from the moors. Cross over to a golf course. Turn 90 degrees right at the edge of the modern housing estate, (one of the few places not posted with the Pendle Way signs). This is a bleak place to practise golf as it is situated on a breezy hill overlooking Burnley. The route beyond the golf course has to be followed carefully to reach the urban community of Reedly and the main road. Here are the first shops since Laneshaw Bridge.

Having played 'death with the traffic', the route takes the walker to the canal and the River Calder, (not the West Yorkshire one). Cross the M65 motorway over a footbridge then pastureland to join the River Calder again on one of its winding valley bends. A long ascent to the right through further farmland eventually reaches

munity life in the vicinity. The barn is reputedly a former monastery, older than the house, where tithes were collected.

From the farm, it is possible to climb up to Foster's Leap, a prominent gritstone rock outcrop and scene of a famous leap by Foster Cunliffe of the Cunliffe family

Pendle Hill from Boulsworth Hill.

Witches Galore, Newchurch in Pendle.

the main road and Higham village. Although on a hillside, Higham is not seen from below nor from above as it soon disappears from view on more upland pasture. A lane leads into a quiet valley seemingly cut off from civilization save for dotted farms and a group of white buildings on the hillside near a plantation. This is Newchurch in Pendle which is aimed for on the well-marked Way through this tranquil rural setting. Newchurch is a 'best kept village', as seen by the plaques on the green border by the toilets. However, its association with witches is perhaps more famous. The Pendle Witches lived in this area during the late sixteenth and early seventeenth centuries. The strongly religious Puritan influence at this time held no favours for witches, who, in reality, though living a 'pagan' life, were very knowledgeable of nature's cures via herbs and other plant potions. Demdike, a witch, was asked to cure a sick cow at Bull Hole below Newchurch. It appears she failed and of course this was used against her, a typical example of the ambivalence held towards witches. Jane and John Bulcock who lived at Moss End, were tried and found guilty of witchcraft in 1612. Nowadays a fascinating shop full of witch paraphernalia is a well-visited place in Newchurch.

The path climbs steeply out of the village over pasture with good angles on Pendle Hill and Barley. Maybe you will see Penyghent in the distance. It goes down by and enters a conifer plantation to emerge at the Ogden Reservoirs. A valley penetrates into the confines of Pendle Hill and is vacated by walking up a spur flanking the beck of Boar Clough. Gradually the hill is conquered. It is a fine viewpoint with bird's-eye views of Barley and far beyond. To seasoned photographers it somehow lacks strong subject matter, however, it is easy to be deceived by the naked eye. George Fox climbed Pendle Hill in 1652, and as the result of a vision, was moved to found the Society of Friends or Quakers. Personally, I was moved towards the lure of a pint at the Pendle Inn in Barley! A steep way down a paved track leads to the whitewashed Pendle House Farm, which

Bird's-eye view over Barley from Pendle Hill.

Lothersdale, a secluded village on the Pennine Way.

catches the light from kilometres away. Above it, when the bracken is dead, is a dark patch. If viewed from some kilometres away, it appears in the shape of a witch! Finally, go over pasture and a fenced track to emerge in Barley.

Further Walking

The ascent of Pendle Hill from Barley via Pendle House, Pendle Hill and Ogden Reservoirs, going in the reverse direction to the Pendle Way. It is about 8 km (5 miles) long.

East of Pendle, in country similar in nature is Lothersdale, a picturesque village cradled in a quiet valley, sleepy, which is seemingly far from the madding crowd, (excepting Pennine Way walkers!). The chimney stack, mill and old cottages set this scene which provides walking possibilities over Pinhaw Beacon, Elslack Reservoir, Carleton, Ravenshaw and Ramshaw Hill, then return. It is 12–14km (8–9 miles) long.

Chapter 6
THE DALES WAY

The Dales Way is an official long-distance path, 130km (81 miles) long from Ilkley to Bowness on Windermere, like the Pennine Way it is a very popular journey. However, it is much shorter and easier than the former, as it utilizes three major rivers, two, the Wharfe and the Dee, being inside much of the Yorkshire Dales. The third is the Lune along the base of the Howgill Fells. West of the M6 motorway, the route has left behind any Pennine hills, and becomes distinctly Cumbrian as it crosses low fells to reach Bowness on Windermere. Important links are possible from major towns in West Yorkshire, and circular day or half-day outings are plentiful using sections of the walk. Rather than repeat what others have so capably written, I shall briefly note points of interest along the route, and alternatives where applicable.

Maps	OS sheet Nos. 97, 98, 104 (1:50,000 series). I recommend the Dales Way Route Guide by Arthur Gemmell and Colin Speakman (Stile Publications, Mercury House, Otley, West Yorkshire LS21 3HE). Maps also available from Footprint, Stirling Enterprises, Stirling FK7 7RP.
Transport	Rail Services: British Rail, Leeds connecting to Ilkley and British Rail at Windermere.
	Bus Services: West Yorks PTE, Metro House, West Parade, Wakefield, West Yorkshire. The Road Car Company Limited of Harrogate, North Yorkshire and Ribble Motor Services (Kendal offices), Cumbria.
Accommodation	West Yorkshire Metropolitan County Council produce a 'Where to Stay' guide, tel: English Tourist Board, 312 Tadcaster Road, York, or the TIC at Piece Hall, Halifax or Hebden Bridge. There are youth hostels in Linton, Grassington, Kettlewell and Dent. Plentiful accommodation means a good choice of distances between the stops and overnights. Beyond the Pennines, check for accommodation through the Cumbria Tourist Board.

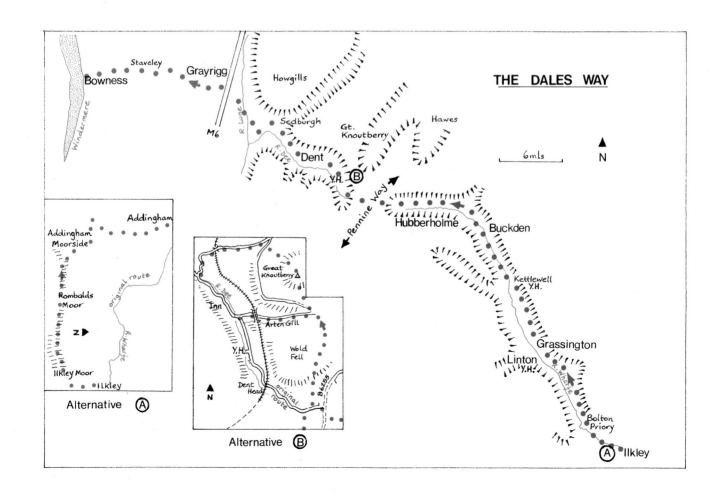

The Dales Way is easily graded. In fact, seasoned hillwalkers may find it monotonously steady, even using muscles they did not realize they had due to long periods of flat walking. Any serious exploration of the Pennines, however, make it a must on the itinerary. The Wharfe can be followed out of Ilkley, but keen walkers can take in Ikley Moor passing the ancient Swastika Stone on the moor top. The elevation gives the taste of the walk to come, as views open up into the higher reaches of Wharfedale. Descend via pastures to Addingham where the choice is to follow the river or go up a green hill with superb views down to Bolton Bridge and the Priory with rolling fells beyond. River walking is the only solution from Bolton Bridge, but Bolton

Bolton Priory, Wharfedale.

The Swastika Stone, an ancient landmark on Ilkley Moor.

Priory must surely warrant a break. Beyond, a permissive path leads into Strid Wood via a tollgate which is now free to non-drivers. The River Wharfe funnels strongly through the narrows at this point, known as 'The Strid', which is reached by an awkward scramble on a low level to the main path. At Barden Bridge there is a bunkhouse and a cafe. Cross the river and commence pasture walking over stiles to reach Burnsall where adequate services are available. The Wharfe leaves the previously enclosed valley to open out in a wide dale where an excellent position is gained with a view of the old church at Linton across the stream. Linton is a pretty village built around a square green with two bridges over a beck. Only 1km (¾ mile) beyond lies Grassington with many shops and services. (Note that the Yorkshire Dales National Park headquarters are in the village.)

Between Grassington and Kettlewell is a fine walk over limestone scenery, with the Conistone Dib – a fine example of a dry valley on the left and good views across Wharfedale towards Kilnsey Crag. Just beyond the Dib is the Conistone Pie, a unique piece of limestone just like a 'Desperate Dan Cow Pie'! The walk slowly descends by small scars to Kettlewell. From Kettlewell, the walk resumes a dales way near the river, with possibilities of a diversion into Starbotton or Buckden villages. The lane and the river lead to Hubberholme, a hamlet with a farm, an inn

Linton village.

The Strid – the gushing narrows of the River Wharfe near Barden.

and a squat-towered church. This gives entry to Langstrothdale where dales scenery is at its best, particularly beyond Yockenthwaite. The River Wharfe trundles down over limestone platforms whilst the Way takes a path adjacent by Deepdale House to reach Beckermonds. There, the Wharfe takes on its name by the joining of

Conistone Dib, a dry limestone valley.

The Conistone Pie, a limestone rock formation.

Buckden village.

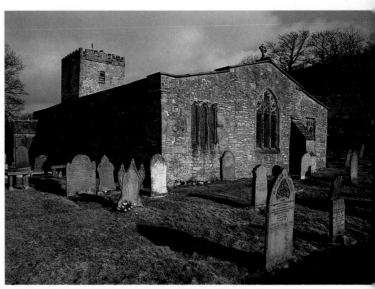

Hubberholme Church.

Evening near Deepdale (Langstrothdale) Dales Way.

Beckermonds, and the infant River Wharfe.

Greenfield and Oughtershaw Becks. The building of Beckermonds stands prominantly at the beck junctions, best illustrated by the photograph.

The minor road to Hawes is followed to Oughtershaw, a collection of farm buildings, and is left for a hardcore track which winds uphill, the destination being Cam Houses, now a bunkhouse, situated high on the moorside at 445m (1,460ft). There are views of High Greenfield Knott and Ingleborough. Beyond Cam Houses, join the Pennine Way until Cam End, to walk to Holme Hill beyond the B6255 road. Alternatively, take a route over a limestone plateau to descend to a hidden valley which gives you wild vistas of Ingleborough, until the B6255 is reached. Personally, I think the latter route is more

Dales Way near Oughtershaw, towards Cam Head.

Summit, Great Knoutberry Fell towards Wild Boar Fell.

commendable, particularly as those long-ing for an ascent can soon bear from the road walk into Dentdale and climb Wold Fell, continuing on to Great Knoutberry Fell, a worthwhile viewpoint over many of the western fells of the Yorkshire Dales. Either descend via the imposing Arten Gill and its viaduct or down the coal road coming over from Garsdale. This depends on whether you are staying at the youth hostel which is situated in a delightful riverside dell. This can also be reached by the ordinary route which simply descends the dale under Denthead viaduct.

Dentdale has a different appearance to most other Yorkshire dales, being well endowed with tree cover and lacking in the profusion of stone walls seen else-where. Instead, hedgerows divide the

enclosures, with the whole scene dare I say, taking on a landscape more reminiscent of the Welsh border hills. The buildings however, are definitely Pennine in character as the walk passes through or by them on spring lines with good meadowland below. There are twists and turns to the path with several ups and downs, on a small scale. Note the availability of a dry or wet weather route along the floor of Dentdale, indeed, I have seen the river burst its banks in several places, even covering the road on the south side of the river downstream of Barth Bridge. The normal route uses this road to Rash and beyond, where it meets and crosses the River Rawthey to go into Millthrop. The latter can be reached on the opposite bank of the Dee from Barth Bridge by going upwards to Mire House and Hewthwaite where field paths open up extensive views

Sportsman Inn, Arten Gill, Arten Viaduct and Great Knoutberry Fell, Dentdale.
Dent village.

Sedbergh with Arant Haw, Howgill Fells, behind.

Runners on Dales Way, Frostrow Fells with Wild Boar Fell beyond.

of the dale, then via the golf course to Sedbergh and the Howgill Fells.

The change in the terrain is caused by the Dent Fault which isolated the carboniferous limestones and gritstones to reveal older Silurian slates and shales, characteristic of Cumbrian Mountains. From Millthrop, either go riverside via the Rawthey, then upstream on the Lune, or go into Sedburgh and out by Howgill Lane to skirt the lower slopes of Winder. These alternatives join beyond Lincoln Bridge near the River Lune. Hole House is a double building split by a yard which takes the walker on round the base of the Howgills to exit the Yorkshire Dales National Park by Crook of Lune Farm. Crook of Lune Bridge is an attractive spot giving a good peek of the Howgill Fells. Note the old railway viaduct and climb a hill to meet and cross over the M6, where, strictly speaking, anything remotely to do with the Pennines has been left behind, and thus does not justify space henceforth.

Chapter 7

THE UFKIL STRIDE

This is an outstanding circuit of fells and dales covering 53km (33 miles) within the Yorkshire Dales National Park. Details of this annual event are in the *Long Distance Walkers' Handbook*. However, it can be done on an individual basis, facilitated by a non-walking, car-driving helper. It can then be done in one, two or even three stages. It is fairly easy to arrange check points with your driver. This can lighten load-carrying and facilitate changes of clothing or footwear. There are no shops on route excepting Buckden's one store, and only the pub in Arncliffe, so careful planning of the walk is essential. It is worth every step of the way.

Maps	The old 1:25,000 series of Malham and Upper Wharfedale. Otherwise, the 1:25,000, Yorkshire Dales Southern, and Yorkshire Dales Northern and Central, OS 1:50,000 series sheet No. 98.
Transport	Railways: Settle to Carlisle. Bus Services: West Yorks PTE, tel: 0756 5331.
Accommodation	*See* Yorkshire Centurion Walk. Also Hawkswick Cote Campsite, tel: 075 677226. Kettlewell Youth Hostel, tel: 075676 232. The start and finish are officially Buckden if you are in the annual event. I recommend Arncliffe if the walk is individually attempted.

Psychologically, two ascents and descents of the same moorland bulk seem better over and done with early in the trek. I refer to the fells separating Littondale and Langstrothdale. Needless to say an early start is essential if attempting the circuit in a day and remember there is 1,500m (5,000ft) of ascent and 1,060m (3,500ft) of descent. By starting from Arncliffe the big

Daybreak, Littondale.

ascents are completed by Fountains Fell, leaving weary legs to wander the steady terrain and long descent into Arncliffe at the end of the day.

Leave Arncliffe to walk to Litton mainly over flat pastureland which could be very wet with dew in the early morning. The route occasionally hugs the River Skirfare and crosses a delightful wooden footbridge

into Litton village to complete the first 3km (2 miles). The village may be still asleep as you pass through noting the post office and the Queen's Head Inn.

Beyond the Queen's Head leave the tarmac road to ascend a cart track which rises steadily giving views as serene as any in the Yorkshire Dales. Traverse an inimitable band of limestone until it gives way to rougher moorland, the track being evident all the way and levelling out with the fine profile of Penyghent seen rising above the dale. The moor head is short and level before a long but rapid descent is made into Upper Wharfedale with Buckden Pike's mass in front and Starbotton huddled at its foot. Meet a drive and walk to the metalled road in order to turn right for Buckden. Climb gently out of Buckden encountering limestone on the Pike's lowest slopes. Double back from near Cray and traverse round a semi-wooded limestone bank with good views down Wharfedale at the same time note the tiny hamlet of Hubberholme below left. Continue to Yockenthwaite where it might be sensible to have the first check point, a cup of tea and a change of footwear (after the wet dew)!

Cross Horsehead Pass by another well

THE UFKIL STRIDE

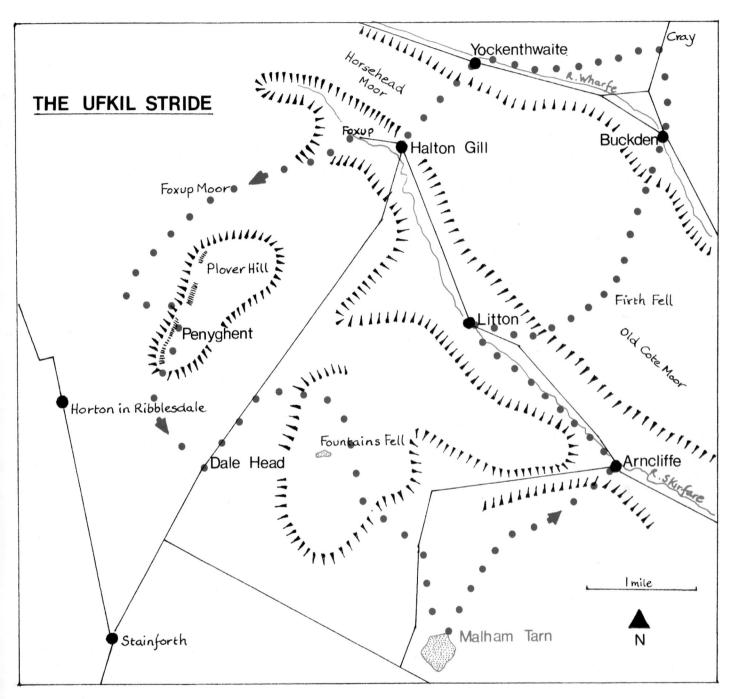

marked track which becomes less demanding than it looks and you will be well-rewarded with superb views to Fountains Fell, Plover Hill and Penyghent. As the Pass dips down, observe the mesa-like top of Ingleborough appearing directly above the hamlet of Foxup. The track twists down to Halton Gill and you carry

on via the metalled road to Foxup. The ascent around the flanks of Plover Hill is in wild but unphotogenic country. I compared the steep pull up Plover Hill to a descriptive word for illegitimacy! Careful negotiation of an almost vertical headwall of grass finally finds respite for lungs, thighs and calves on a level moor from

which a rapid recovery in pace is made for a couple of kilometres to Penyghent (which is boggy in wet weather). Fine vistas of Upper Ribblesdale appear with Ingleborough and Whernside as focal points.

Legions of walkers visit the summit of Penyghent which has beggar-like sheep

Litton, Littondale and Penyghent.

Fountains Fell from Horse Head Pass.

Foxup and Ingleborough behind.

who will even stoop to theft of food from your rucksack if you are not aware. Here, is a Pennine mountain with position and shape. Wild fell country leads east to Fountains Fell and beyond to Buckden Pike and Great Whernside. To the west, Ingleborough dominates, as does Whernside but to a lesser extent. To the south, the dales fall away and rise at a distance with the Bowland moors, to the left of which Pendle Hill is prominent and even the South Pennines beyond, if clarity permits. The hill itself falls away and is trunkated into rims of geological time exposure, and the rims ahead, on its left flank are descended. Duckboards facilitate progress and abate erosion as the slopes become gentler. Swing round by Churn Milk Hole a circular chasm (which might

be re-named 'Litter Hole'), to follow the Pennine Way to the road pass. Here, have a second check point.

Follow the Pennine Way north to south over Fountains Fell, an easier climb than it looks. The track leaves out the true summit which is about several hundred metres right amid peat hags and tussocky grasses. Keep an eye on the route, for even the Pennine Way is not so well worn on Fountains Fell. It makes a protracted descent to meet the Arncliffe–Malham road. Still follow the Pennine Way to reach Malham Tarn, a final check point.

Malham Tarn is set in a 1,740-hectare (4,300-acre) estate, which belongs to the National Trust. It is the highest lime-rich lake in England at 375m (1,230ft). The tarn sits on a saucer-shaped base of Silurian

Buckden Pike and Great Whernside seen from Penyghent.

Churn Milk Hole and Penyghent.

The Three Peaks of Yorkshire from Fountains Fell.

Evening overlook of Malham Tarn.

rock which is impervious to water and hemmed in by glacial material – thus it is rich in nutrients and holds varied and sometimes unique flora and fauna. The wild flowers include Mountain Pansy, and Mealy Primrose. Indigenous birds include Great Crested Grebe, Coot, Mallard and Common Sandpiper. The Tarn House Field Centre situated here, was a former shooting lodge once visited by Charles Kingsley, who after seeing the area was inspired to write *The Water Babies*.

The last part of this sojourn takes the walker from Malham Tarn over Great Close Scar's flanks into a secluded valley passing by a lonely building. Another abandoned building is passed set in its clump of trees, then you contour the fell for nearly 5km (3 miles). This part of the journey is

Rowan, Yew Cogar Scar.

Above Arncliffe.

Limestone walls and barn, Malhamdale.

memorable for the sweeping views and the obstacle course of ladder stiles – just what the doctor ordered at the end of such a hike! However, it does reserve for you the finale of Yew Cogar Scar, a spectacular limestone ravine with its water course leading into Arncliffe. Keep to the path above this abyss and hopefully, the late afternoon sun will give low direct lighting towards Arncliffe, enhancing the barns and drystone wall patterns of Littondale which is ultimately gained by a twisting descent, to end one of the finest walks in the Pennines.

Further Walking

1   Malham, Janet's Foss, Gordale Scar

The entrance to Goredale Scar.

Malham Cove.

(tricky ascent), Malham Tarn, Malham Lings and Malham Cove return.

2   Threshfield, Wood Nook, Bordley, Mastiles lane, Kilnsey. (Either take a car to Kilnsey beforehand or catch a bus back, or the fit can walk via Conistone and Grassington return.)

3   Buckden, Buckden Pike, Starbotton Fell, Starbotton, Dales Way return.

South of Grassington, a fine walk starts and finishes from Barden Bridge, on the River Wharfe. Follow the Dales Way to Howgill, turning right to cross the minor road and upwards to zigzag into woods. Emerge from these to turn left over the fell to Simon's Seat, a magnificent viewpoint. Turn southwards to Great Aygill Head to cross the beck, then follow it all the way down through the Valley of Desolation to Waterfall Cottage. A path on the east bank of the Wharfe leads above The Strid via woods, and then back to Barden Bridge.

Chapter 8

AN INTRODUCTION TO LIMESTONE

Although the Ufkil Stride (Chapter 7) is in limestone country, the three walks which follow are classical samplers of what this rock has to offer. The largest area of British limestone scenery occurs in the north of England, between Morecambe Bay in the west, Richmond in the east, Settle in the south and the Milburn Forest in the north. These rocks consist of many pavements left as smooth sheets of rock, because of the scouring action of ice age movements (sometimes with gritstone passengers as at Norber). Water has dissolved and removed limestone along cracks and joints called grikes leaving individual paving stones called clints. The clint surfaces are often runnelled by drainage. The pavements are stunning in their architecture and support an abundance of flora and fauna. The need for their conservation is paramount and some therefore have become National Nature Reserves providing wonderful places to wander.

Attermire Scar (Circuit)

A fine walk visiting the sylvan riverside of the Ribble, Stainforth village, and the outstanding limestone scenery above and beyond Langcliffe where the 'Alps' of Attermire Scar and Warrendale Knotts give loftier images of far away Italian mountains.

Maps OS 1:50,000 series sheet No. 98. The 1:25,000 series showing the Yorkshire Dales Southern Section, or the Old Malham and Upper Wharfedale map.

You start and finish at Settle.

Settle stands stout and proud as a gateway town to Upper Ribblesdale, backed by the limestone crag of Castleburgh. The Shambles in the centre is a fine piece of architecture and two nearby car parks provide a starting point. Walk down the main road westwards to where it crosses the River Ribble, there you gain a path to the right which skirts playing fields and crosses enclosures and reaches a minor road going towards Little Stainforth. Keep to this road until you reach a wide track to the right which goes back to the riverside by a

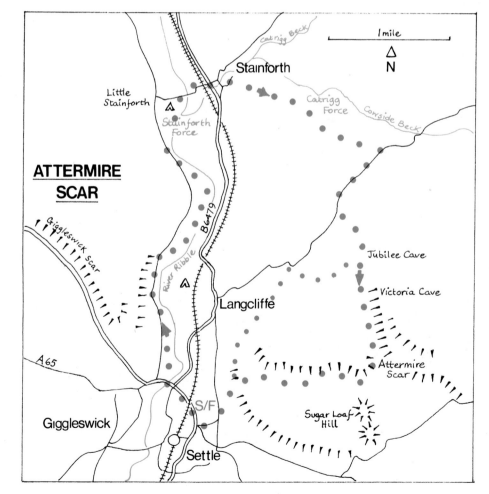

Pack-horse Bridge, River Ribble, Stainforth.

Victoria Cave (Attermire Scar).

weir. From here go to Stainforth Bridge. The path is quite delightful as first it leads the eye to the chimney and mill on the opposite bank, then having turned the corner, the green pasture and tree-lined river provide a pretty walk. Stainforth Force, a three-tiered waterfall lies in the beginnings of a mini-gorge, yet a few metres upstream, the water is placid as it flows beneath the single-arched pack-horse bridge which is in turn delicately negotiated by motorists visiting the adjacent caravan and camping park. The lane is taken to cross the main road into Stainforth which has a café and a pub.

To leave Stainforth, take Goat Scar Lane, a typical walled dales thoroughfare that climbs steeply then more gently upwards. A wooded gill is hidden on the

Warrendale Knotts and Attermire Scar.

left, and it makes a very worthwhile visit in order to admire the hidden Catrigg Force – a substantial waterfall making two drops from a craggy amphitheatre. Go back up and over the stile to turn up a field and pick up a track along Langcliffe Scar which gives views down to the Ribble Valley below. This meets a minor road. Continue in the same line on a green path into open limestone country, but be careful to locate a ladder stile in a wall up to the left. Having gone over this, make a short excursion uphill to visit Jubilee Cave – the adventurous may find it possible to creep and crawl through the cave, to emerge through a 'window' on a higher level. Several hundred metres away, having

regained the track along the back of a wall, the limestone scar is now of quite impressive proportions. It supports Victoria Cave, a much larger hole in the limestone face. Both these caves were discovered on the Jubilee Day of Queen Victoria, hence their names.

Descend with care from Victoria Cave and proceed along the base of the scar where the path goes down between crags left and right. Look along each way to admire the well-sculptured limestone cliffs, particularly those now more close at hand, Warrendale Knotts which look like small versions of the Dolomites.

Having explored or lingered in this worthwhile location, either proceed up

around the flank of the main hill, parallel to the main track below, or use the track itself. Either way joins up, to head back towards Settle. Suddenly, a roof-top view over Settle and Giggleswick appears, the track descends with fine views all the way until the edge of the town is entered via narrow ginnels or lanes to return to the start.

Norber, Crummackdale and Moughton

A walk where atmosphere is the keynote. The landscape of Norber and Crummack Dale is almost surrealistic. Glacial erratics, followed by supreme limestone architecture are located in wild expanses, evoking the imagination.

Map   1:50,000, No. 98 and 1:25,000 the Old Three Peaks, or Yorkshire Dales Southern Section.

I have taken this walk three times to date, and frankly, if I lived nearby, I might take it every week. Starting and finishing at Austwick the route goes uphill past well-appointed dwellings at Townhead. The metalled lane reaches a junction where you join a green lane to the left, and you soon vacate this by a signed path to Norber. The brow of this hill and that of Robin Proctor Scar lie ahead over green pasture. Although Robin Proctor Scar draws the eye, if you keep right of it and wind your way up the short steep gradient, the as yet undisclosed secrets of Norber will be found.

Here, on the shoulder of the landscape many gritstone boulder erratics are perched, lying, sometimes precariously on plinths of limestone underneath. Glaciers of the last ice age defied gravity by sweeping over this brow and depositing their Silurian passengers on top of limestone clints. The more moronic of the human race have stooped to deface some of these specimens with graffiti. The field of boulders is extensive and just to come here might be enough for some. Others will proceed over the ladder stile in the corner of the wall up the hill. This will lead to more fascination.

Keeping above a limestone wall, a feint track contours the hillside with a slight rise over limestone scree. Crummack Farm lies just out of sight in the trees below and to the right. The dale is quiet and serene, flanked by the capping limestone of Moughton with the imposing Penyghent beyond. Ahead, some undula-

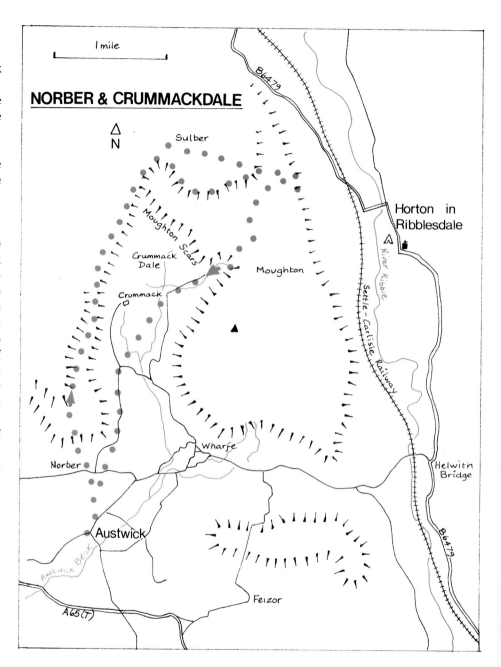

tions and small groups of clints are traversed upwards to a green plateau which is joined by paths from Clapham and Crummack Farm. On the left the flat-topped Ingleborough broods. A large cairn breaks an otherwise endless horizon, but soon this leads to a gate, called 'Sulber Gate' on the map. 'Centurion' walkers pass here. Although the turn right leads

over the canyon rim, it is well worth a potter into the upper fan of limestone called 'Thieves Moss' simply to be at close quarters to this primaeval landscape. Wander to the nick in the second canyon rim, known as 'Beggars' Stile' which overlooks the green dale of Crummack with views of Pendle Hill beyond which stands alone in what could only be an English pastoral scene.

Having regained the upper rim, plod round it for some distance and keep heading towards Penyghent. You are on an Iron Age path known as 'Sulber Nick' which is well worn into the limestone. It is necessary to find a fence and follow it right to pick up a path on to Moughton. Here, are the last vestiges of Juniper trees forcing a stunted growth in the exposed terrain. Having been to Arizona, I dare to say that these wilds remind me of the American West, however, this is an entirely personal feeling! It is hard to imagine that just out of sight is the ugly quarry works below Moughton Hill.

Now turn right, and you will see the key which is another nick in the limestone where the way twists down into Crummack Dale passing by a shooting box and

Barn, Austwick.

Barn, Robin, Proctor Scar, North Yorkshire.

Glacial erratic. Gritstone upon limestone, Norber.

Crummackdale and Moughton.

on into the walled Moughton Lane. It is possible to wander off right to see the stream emergence at Austwick Beck Head. The footpath finally crosses enclosures

Penyghent from Thieves Moss, Crummackdale.

to meet a vehicular lane of hardcore going to and from Crummack Farm. Go down to White Stone Lane, then go right, and immediately across fields, then turn left to join the original lane into Austwick. Look across and back at Moughton, and I wonder, if like me, you will feel a hankering to return to the environs of Crummack Dale.

Ingleton, White Scars, Chapel-le-Dale, Scales Moor, Thornton Force, Pecca Falls

Maps OS 1:50,000, No. 98, showing Wensleydale and Upper Wharfedale. 1:25,000 series old Three Peaks, or Yorkshire Dales Southern Area No. 10.

There is no need to climb Ingleborough on this walk, though further exertion and time will allow for it. Rather, enjoy the limestone scars and pavements on a circuit which has an air of expansive loneliness, until you reach the contrasting sylvan falls area.

Starting from Ingleton, where there is a free car-park, proceed as if climbing Ingleborough on the trade route via Crina Bottom. A half a kilometre before Crina Bottom, cross a ladder stile and turn left on to the limestone hill from where a green track is picked up. This track becomes indistinct later, but you can find the way by skirting the extensive pavements on their right, under the brow of Ingleborough which presents a different shape from hereabouts. It is worth a saunter on to the Southerscales pavements to admire their jigsaw patterns, and if it is spring, their plant species which

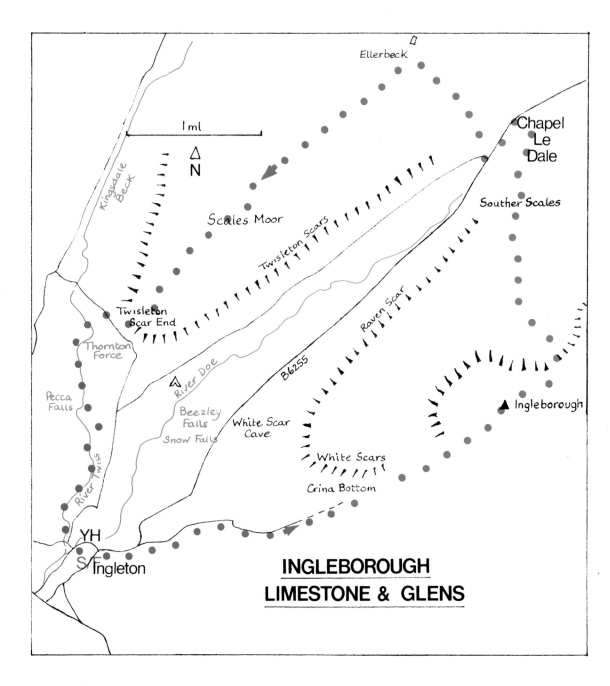

Limestone pavement, Southerscales near Chapel-le-Dale.

Thornton Force, Ingleton Glens.

nestle in the shelter of the grike clefts. Gnarled trees somehow get their living from the cracks in this rocky platform. On the edge of Southerscales, observe the well-trodden path coming down from Ingleborough and join it to twist down below the outcropping limestone and walk on a green path that levels to meet the road. The Old Hill Inn provides drinks and snacks.

From the pub, go down the road to turn first available right up a lane, passing St Leonard's Church and a curious modern sculpture which looked to me like a skeleton. The lane emerges from the trees on to the moor and a signposted track is taken to the left. The Ribblehead Viaduct is prominent behind you, until the track, having climbed almost imperceptibly,

Ingleborough from Twisleton Scar.

levels out and more limestone pavements are encountered. The track becomes indistinct, but by keeping the boundary wall about 200 metres to your right, you may find a couple of very curious fan-like limestone swallow holes on either side of your route. Soon, you will find you clamber down Twisleton Scar End to find a better green track which winds down to the base of the hill. Take a right turn here and note a sign pointing the way to the waterfalls.

The waterfall Thornton Force when in spate is reminiscent of a smaller version of High Force. There is a ticket kiosk to enter the private grounds on a paved path. Pecca Falls is passed in several plunges. Continue in this wooded glade and gorge in delightful surroundings until the land suddenly opens up and a lane to the left leads back to Ingleton.

Chapter 9

THE YORKSHIRE DALES CENTURION WALK

This is 160km (100 miles) of strenuous but classic walking, circumnavigating the major dales and outer fells of the Yorkshire Dales National Park. This walk is not for the casual or inexperienced walker! It was first devised by Jonathan Ginesi whose *Adventure Plan* is published by John Siddall Printers Limited, Horncastle Street, Cleckheaton, West Yorkshire BD19 3JL. This booklet is not a guide. It leaves the planning to the individual. However, I shall attempt to offer some insight into this outstanding journey.

Maps	OS 1:50,000 series sheet Nos. 91, 92, 97 and 98. The 1:25,000 Outdoor Leisure series Nos. 2, 10 and 30. Note however, that Howgill Fells is not completely shown. Therefore, check availability of Harvey Map Services Limited who had a map exclusive to the Howgills. Unfortunately, at time of writing they had gone from their former address and were 'not known'.
Transport	Rail Services at Settle/Carlisle, telephone any major British Rail station.
	Bus Services to and from Whaites, Settle or Horton, tel: 07292 3235 or 3446.
Accommodation	There are guest houses at Horton in Ribblesdale, Dent, Kings Head, Ravenstonedale, Tan Hill Inn and there is Grinton Lodge Youth Hostel or guest houses in Reeth, as well as Aysgarth Youth Hostel or guest houses and finally Kettlewell Youth Hostel or guest houses. For the guest houses, telephone the Yorkshire Dales National Park on: 04865 419.

The start and finish is at Horton in Ribblesdale.

This is a wild country walk necessitating fitness and navigation skills. There are considerable stretches over 450m (1,500ft). Full clothing and equipment is necessary to the same degree as for mountain walking. Instead of crossing the moorland between Tan Hill and Langthwaite, an alternative route can be taken, walking the Pennine Way to Keld, then either the Coast to Coast walk to Reeth, or the beautiful Swaledale to Gunnerside walk followed by the terraces above to Reeth.

The Yorkshire Dales Centurion Walk

Day 1

Horton in Ribblesdale is a fragmented settlement made up of two strands of ribbon development hugging the B6479 road, 10km (6 miles) north of Settle. The Settle/Carlisle railway threads through the

From Ingleborough towards Penyghent, Fountains Fell and Great Whernside.

YORKSHIRE DALES CENTURION WALK

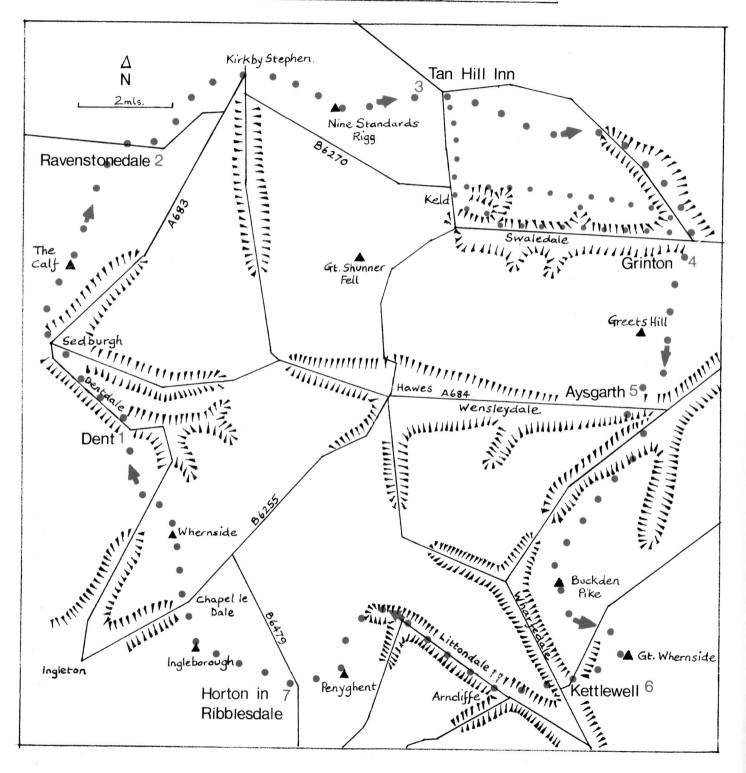

west side and the whole scene is jarred by the quarry works at the foot of an otherwise attractive area of limestone scars and pavements. This is Moughton, which has to be crossed as the first noteworthy landscape feature. The ascent of the scars flattens out to a level wilderness with Ingleborough in front and Penyghent behind. Like sleeping dinosaurs, they are bulky above the wild sweeps of the dale. A small canyon rim is traversed. This is the head of Crummack Dale but it is named Sulber Nick. A final tree stands stout from the limestone clints defiant to this exposed wilderness. Ahead, and dwarfed by the sweep of Ingleborough is a shooting box. A steady climb is made to this point, where you will notice how the vegetation

has changed underfoot in the transition from limestone to a more acidic soil under which are layers of shale and grit. There are duckboards to alleviate erosion from the more boggy surfaces of this long steady climb up the mountain. A col with a final ridge on the left gives way to Ingleborough's summit plateau, which has two cairns, the larger being cross-shaped and pointing to the prime compass points, a handy attribute in mist. Views extend to Morecambe Bay, the Lakeland peaks and along the Pennine whalebacks to the north-west and north-east if the weather is clear.

Retrace your steps to the col, but then follow the sweeping rim of the mountain around part of Simon Fell, in order to drop steeply into the nature reserve of South-

erscales. Beware of cutting downhill too early in mist as the slopes are potentially dangerous. It is tempting to explore the superb pavements of Southerscales, but this can be done on another occasion, and besides, it is a long way to Dent. However, refreshment can be taken at the Old Hill Inn. Don't let the beer go to your head as the next barrier is Whernside!

A paved road from Chapel-le-Dale leads to the limestone of Bruntscar and a zigzag track presents a sign, 'Footpath to Whernside – 1¾ miles'. These are Yorkshire miles and in what seems like 3 of them, meander up the huge scarp to eventually find the steps put in the fellside to save erosion. Whoever laid these must have had a 45-in inside leg measurement, which

Ingleborough from Southerscales.

From Southerscales to Whernside.

Great Knoutberry Fell from Whernside.

has defeated their object because people are easing the groin strain by walking either side of them – *ad erosion infiniteum!* A steep cairned ascent leads to the summit, the highest in the Dales. This can be a bracing position. Ingleborough is isolated and mesa-like in a bleak wilderness which appears much vaster than it really is. Below, the Ribblehead Viaduct makes a lead-in to Penyghent. Further fells, notably Great Knoutberry Fell with a rail viaduct beneath, hold the gaze. From the trig point across the wall, a descent to the pass of White Shaw Moss gives splendid views of Deepdale with the Howgill Fells behind. Take the walled lane a few hundred metres up the road. It can get tedious after wet weather in just under a kilometre where it virtually disappears in bog. Trail bike intrusions have accentuated divots and made deep runnels, adding to the tedium. This can be a despairing place in mist, but clear weather will hold the prospect of Dentdale ahead, as you interminably contour the slopes of Great Coum on this 'occupation' road. The right turn into Flintergill is welcomed by a descent into this rowan-decked limestone gulch which leads directly into Dent village. Accommodation is plentiful, but it is advisable to book well in advance, because of the attraction of this beautiful cobblestoned village – a gem of the Yorkshire Dales.

Dent held more importance than Sedbergh because the polling station for this district was located here until 1863. But the demise of its market had started in the 1830s and declined, even though it struggled on to the late nineteenth century. The town had thrived on the knitting industry from Elizabethan times, and was a self-sufficient, productive, industrial and farming community, that was disrupted by the Industrial Revolution and was saved in part by the building of the Settle/Carlisle Railway. Dent's most famous son, Adam Sedgwick (1785–1873) was born at the parsonage and became professor of geology at Cambridge University. He is immortalized in the prominent stone in the main street.

Day 2

From Dent, the Dales Way is followed on a riverside path which is gained outside the village. This leads to Barth Bridge. Although the Dales Way goes to Sedbergh, our route takes on the Frostrow Fells that separate Garsdale from Dentdale, and, as the climb is made by a walled lane, then a green lane, it permits views back into Dentdale. Go up to the open moor through a fold, here it becomes a grassy track which follows a wall over the bracken-strewn fell. The terrain then becomes hillocky, and difficulty might be had in keeping direction because numerous sheep tracks confuse the issue. However, the weather has to be very bad not to see Sedbergh and part or all of the Howgill Fells behind. Look out for Hollins and Lane Ends on the map, as these settlements will guide you into Sedbergh. This fine town which is Norse in origin, lies on ancient routes from Kendal to York and Lancaster to Newcastle. It spreads its dwellings along the foot of the prominent hill called 'Winder'. And the huddle of buildings along the main cobbled shopping street gives an intimate atmosphere. There may be time for refreshment here. If so, a small café along the main street is recommended. See if they still do 'Wickey Wockey Pudding'. Those who dare try it are in for a delight!

The traverse of the Howgills beckons. Although inside the National Park, these grassy fells are composed of metamorphic rock and appear like outsiders to the fells of the rest of the Dales. However, their crossing can be sheer delight as the Cumbrian Mountains, to which they are geologically closer related, are beautifully displayed to the west, while Cross Fell and the Duns can be seen from The Calf to the north. The going underfoot is usually good. If mist cloaks these fells, it is better to go by lanes and tracks on the low slopes of the Rawthey Valley, diverting over a minor road at Nainthwaite and over the fell to Ravenstonedale.

Otherwise, it is out of Sedbergh by the toilets to a green path which goes right

On the Howgills across to Lakeland (the Cumbrian Mountains).

From the Calf down Langdale Beck with Cross Fell in the distance.

above Settlebeck Gill to flank Arant Haw before undulating on to Calders and then The Calf, at 677m (2,220ft) this is the highest fell in the Howgills. Mind you don't trip up as your eye continuously strays to the superb vistas. Pace down into the seclusion of Bowerdale Beck, a classic V-shaped valley penetrating deep into the fells, then get your breath for the uphill pant on to Randygill Top for another open undulating fell walk over Green Bell and Knoutberry from whose descent a track is picked up near Wyegarth Gill. Cross this and keep to the right of a walled enclosure, in order to find the lane into Ravenstonedale.

Ravenstonedale is a charming village seemingly miles from anywhere – well, it is really! The stonework of the village terraces is decidedly Cumbrian grey. As the lane bisects the cottages, swing round left and pass through the churchyard to reach The Kings Head Hotel, a recommended overnight stop with a friendly atmosphere as well as good food and facilities. From this inn, there are regular fox hunts into the Smardale Fells. They are foot hunts which implies there are no horses used. For those who enjoy this activity, check at the hotel for further details. These events, despite any controversy, are very popular with the locals.

Day 3

The sequestered nooks of Ravenstonedale hide it from the suprisingly near main road, the A685. Locate the A685 and cross it to reach a path which traverses pasture to link up with The Coast to Coast Walk at Smardale Bridge. Take the cart track rightwards up the hawthorn-spattered hillside to reveal the Smardale Viaduct which is now disused, below. Behind, is the graceful outline of the Howgill Fells, and the gap of Smardale Beck reveals the backcloth of the Lune Forest Fells. Notice the several raised mounds of ancient man-made origin on the hillside. Now the open moor of Smardale Fell heralds a good stride where the scene extends to Cross Fell and the skyline masts of Great Dun Fell's tracking station. Ahead, Nine Standards Rigg, Mallerstang Edge and Wild Boar Fell, sprawl behind the intervening Eden Valley.

Your peaceful progress might be interrupted by the whine of A10 Thunderbolts, zig-zagging along the Eden Valley. I'm a sucker for low-flying jets – just a kid at heart, oohing and aahing at their speed, power and agility – not a sentiment shared with some locals or indeed, my wife!

A protracted but pretty descent goes via three railway line bridges, one being the Settle–Carlisle line, the others being long disused. The actual Coast to Coast route is complicated, so it is quicker to go via road from Waitby past a detached former schoolhouse to find a footpath signed 'Bloody Bones Lane'. The more pastoral lowlands lead by Kirkby Stephen Grammar School, in whose fields, girls

might be playing hockey. The town affords a welcome break with cafés and chip shops to tempt the palate. The parish church of St Stephen gives a clue to the town's name. On occasions, the town bustles with farm vehicles and four-wheel-drive motors attending a 'tup' or sheep sale.

The walk exits the elongated town at the market place down a twisted back lane to cross the young yet substantial River Eden via Franks Bridge which is perhaps a suitable spot for an artist. The route goes over dairy land now as the way leads to Hartley, with a stream bisecting the pretty cottages. Careful map checks lead to the quarry road and a stiff gradient.

Look right if you must at the quarry eyesores. Eventually, the climb relents and a green bridleway goes to Nine Standards Rigg. The Nine Standards or cairns can be picked out, but being larger than humans, they belie the distance to them. We were able to enjoy fine weather at these cairns with extensive panoramas, however, Nine Standards Rigg can be a dreary place in mist. It is possible to go across the very rough moor directly to Tan Hill, but there is no official right of way here. Much before you appears a vast desert of peat hags, heather, grass tufts and bog, with the slight whaleback of Rogan's Seat the only rise across the

Smardale Viaduct and Lune Forest beyond.

Kirkby Stephen and St Stephen's Church.

Nine Standards Rigg, (The Nine Standards).

Tan Hill Inn, highest pub in Britain, stands alone in a moorland waste.

wilderness. Rogan, whoever he was, might have picked a better place to sit!

As Tan Hill is the objective, the burden of choice lies before the walker to go direct – over who knows what – or to follow the circuitous Coast to Coast route to Raven Seat and turn north-east towards the inn. This is a choice between the devil and the deep blue sea! Either way, it is a unique experience to visit or stay overnight at the Tan Hill Inn, protected by the famous double glazing, warm fires and good food at Britain's highest hostelry, 528m (1,732ft) above sea level.

Day 4

Today presents a difficult choice of routes. I am never averse to making a walk more attractive. Therefore, if you wish to avoid

further moorland complexities, perhaps follow the Pennine Way to Keld, then the Coast to Coast trail up Swinnergill, East Grain and Gunnerside Gill to Reeth. Although moors are crossed, they are facilitated by the use of miner's tracks. In bad conditions go by Muker, to follow the Swale to Gunnerside, then the fellside to Reeth. Note that either of these routes are more scenic than the purists way which crosses the bulge of Water Crag on a badly drained moorland track to Great Punchard Head and Gill. It improves hereon to Arkengarthdale. But despite a beautiful day, I only began to enjoy the day's walk on reaching Arkengarthdale.

Cross Arkle Beck at the hamlet of Whaw and follow it down to Langthwaite

Arkengarthdale.

Langthwaite, Arkengarthdale.

through a small plantation and across a minor road keeping to the east side all the way. Langthwaite is attractive and has an inn for refreshment. Admire the towered church which is a focal point of the dale. Arkle Beck is followed for a further 5km (3 miles) as it flanks Fremington Edge, continuing in the vein of pleasant riverside walking all the way to Reeth. Some 'Centurion' walkers may have time to carry on over the moors via Grinton and Castle Bolton to Aysgarth. However, even in the best of conditions, walking is a heads down business, the greater distance you undertake, the more likely you'll be looking at your feet rather than the super scenery. With this pressure there is no time to stop and take in the atmosphere of a place. Yet the 'Centurion' cries out for

Castle Bolton, Wensleydale.

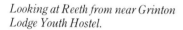

Looking at Reeth from near Grinton Lodge Youth Hostel.

this. Therefore, it would be good to stay overnight in Reeth or Grinton giving you time to enjoy either of these places. The following day would then be easy, reaching only as far as Aysgarth, but allowing for a look around Castle Bolton and the falls at Aysgarth.

Aysgarth Falls.

Alternative No 1 Day 4

Follow the Pennine Way to Keld, but do not cross the river. There is a sign denoting the Coast to Coast trail. Turn left and follow this. Note the sylvan waterfalls of Catrake and Kisdon Forces. The path

trends uphill to the ruins of Crackpot Hall which gives glimpses of Keld along the wooded ravine which has been carved out by the River Swale. Crackpot Hall, a former farmhouse stands forlorn. Obviously it was not abandoned for its aspect which is impressive as the Swale snakes downstream along a flat-bottomed valley framed by Kisdon Hill and Ivelet Moor.

The path aims left contouring the hill with Swinnergill's hidden gorge below. Cross a bridge to the right by a scenic waterfall of the East Grain Beck which is followed uphill by a ruined smelt mill. Look back and see Great Shunner Fell behind the valley sides. Two hundred or more metres of questionable footpath in boggy terrain lead to the open moor joining a vehicular track which has sadly scarred

East Grain, beyond Swinnergill to Great Shunner Fell. (The Centurion alternative route No. 1.)

Gunnerside, Swaledale and Great Shunner Fell. (The Centurion alternative route No. 2.)

In Swinnergill, Swaledale Area.

the hillside of Ivelet Moor. Now make excellent progress to Gunnerside Gill, observing the ruins of Blakethwaite Smelt Mill. Turn sharp left into the valley or 'hush' to ascend up the other side. Thanks to man's intrusion, a ruinous moor of gravel, spoil and hardcore is traversed to Hard Level Gill and further ruins. However, it is now a pleasant walk along the gill to Surrender Bridge, then over

Hard Level Gill.

Cringley Bottom's tricky ravine. Finally, enjoy an elevated walk over green limestone pastures past a couple of farms to Reeth. As you walk look back up Swaledale and enjoy its beautiful aspect.

Alternative No 2 Day 4

Follow the Pennine Way to Keld, then walk over the superb hill of Kisdon, in the possible company of attendant lapwings. Proceed to Muker, leaving it for riverside pasture walking. Cross the Swale by an excursion upstream to a wooden bridge commanding a fine aspect of river and hill landscape. Following the Swale to Gunnerside is easy and the walk through numerous meadows and gap stiles is delightful. A pause should be made to admire the arch of Ivelet Bridge, before a couple of kilometres of further pastures enclosed by drystone walls leads to Gunnerside – a gem of a settlement with a good pub!

Leaving eastwards on the B-road, the route takes a green cart track that ascends the fell. This is the point to admire the intrinsic pattern of barns and field enclosures on the riverside pastures below. Head for the hamlet of Blades, being careful to keep on the fellside to meet up with further smatterings of dwellings and barns by Kearton. Cross the lane and in a couple of kilometres, cross the bridge of Barney Beck. Go via Thiernswood Hall and keep to the contour to Riddings and thence to Reeth, at the end of a wonderful day's walking.

Day 5

There is now a chance to slow down the hitherto strenuous schedule. Take the chance to look more closely at Reeth with its vantage point over Arkle Beck and the verdant Swale and admire the village green on a square, bisected by the snaking road. Perhaps you can visit the Folk Museum. Then study the map as there are two ways to leave. One is over a bridge on the Swale to the west, aiming for Dyke House and Harkerside Moor, to meet the unfenced road at a high point of 387m (1,270ft). The other route follows the road to Grinton, (where you may have decided to stay at the youth hostel). You then travel uphill to the same high point. There is a lovely view back to Reeth showing its layout on the end of the promontory. The well-marked moorland path is easy going but not intimately scenic. However, your gaze may be attracted as far as the North Yorks Moors and Cleveland Hills across the flat Vale of Mowbray on a clear day. Go by Greets Hill quarry (disused), along a bridleway which, after the crossing of another near stream junctions, slowly descends the heather moor and lands straight in Castle Bolton.

Castle Bolton is an eye-catching fortress picked out by the observant from several points in Wensleydale. It was built by Richard Scope, a veteran of the Battle of Crecy and was constructed between 1379 and 1397. Mary Queen of Scots was imprisoned here between 1568 and 1569.

On the way down to this notable monument, the wide sweeps of Wensleydale open up; their width giving perhaps less intimacy than the narrower Swaledale. Departing behind the castle, look for a clump of trees across the pasture of the first enclosure. This gives a gentle descent to Carperby. First pass the farm buildings of West Bolton before rounding a copse on its north side. Further barns are negotiated before the village is entered. The houses hug the solitary road, splitting this peaceful place before a left turn is taken between dwellings to new pastures that lead to the woods surrounding Aysgarth Falls. Depending on the season, the flora of this woodland should be seen carpeting its floors. Refreshments and tourist information perhaps call for a lengthier interlude, before gaining access to the upper falls which are seldom without human admirers at hand. Then find your pre-determined accommodation at a youth hostel, guest house or inn in this village which is curiously split into two sections; the first around the falls and the second a kilometre to the west.

Day 6

One hundred metres west of the inn in the west end of the village, a path wends its way south and east, crossing gap stiles in the walled enclosures to pass over a lea and descend into Thoralby. Ahead, Pennine fells sprawl either side of the long corridor of Bishopdale. Carry on through

The Three Peaks from Buckden Pike.

Newbiggin, and just about the last dwelling of this village is a cottage dated 1690. Strike uphill on a cart truck and ignore the OS map, in order to keep the track as seen, it rises through Newbiggin Pasture by a solitary tree, before climbing through a miniature limestone scar on to the level of Wasset Fell. Fine panoramas abound over Bishopdale with the Wensleydale fells behind. Lady Wasset Well, though

marked on the map is a pointless search, so plod on by ruined buildings on to a boggy moorland track over the extensive Naughtberry Hill and Buckden Pike. Having no outstanding feature at hand, it is hoped fair weather will give a straightforward, isolated walk along this high Pennine whaleback ridge. The gradient stiffens to the summit of Buckden Pike, hardly a true summit in the proper sense

Great Whernside summit towards Buckden Pike.

of the word, but wild vistas compensate, with Great Whernside to the south-east and the Three Peaks and Fountains Fell to the west. Now grit your teeth for the prospect ahead, for you must descend the moor over Tor Mere Top and Tor Dike earthwork, then cross the minor road pass to slog up Great Whernside. Once aloft on this great mound, you will experience a grassier carpet underfoot with gritstone slabs and boulders to interest the eye on the scarp edge. Go to the other flank of the broad ridge and look down over part of Angram Reservoir. From the trig point at 703m (2,308ft), make the best way downhill, aiming for Hag Dyke and then pick up a better path to reach a lane into Kettlewell, whose hostel and guest houses offer accommodation. Slow walkers could descend direct from Buckden Pike over Top Mere Road, a green walled lane, into Kettlewell. Kettlewell is mentioned in the Domesday Book, and was once more important than Grassington.

Dawn over Angram and Scar House Reservoirs (Great Whernside).

Above Kettlewell, Wharfedale.

Fellscape west from Penyghent.

Day 7

Leave Kettlewell by a cart track that starts across the bridge over the River Wharfe. Leave this almost immediately for a climb towards a nick in the limestone scar above. Having a rest and getting your breath back at this point enables you to have a bird's-eye view over Kettlewell and the grid patterns of drystone walls sweeping across the dale below. Level out on a moor, until, dipping, the lush green Littondale lies ahead and below. Descend through a wood and limestone rocks to enter Arncliffe. Follow the dale bottom scene for a few kilometres up to Halton Gill. The Ufkil Stride shares part of the walk between Arncliffe and Litton, then from Halton Gill, Foxup, and around Plover Hill. The Centurion Way, however, chooses to miss out this fell and heads for the gaping abyss of Hull Pot, following the Pennine Way to Penyghent, whose summit is described in Chapter 7.

Descending from the rocky tiers of Penyghent, there is, where the path levels out, another path to the right. This leads very pleasantly towards the farm of Brackenbottom, with Ribblesdale stretched laterally in front.

Walk into Horton to complete the superb round walk of 'The Centurion' which is surely one of the best circular walks in Britain!

Penyghent from the Pennine Way approach.

Alternative Day 7

Walkers could ease the final day's efforts by climbing a well-marked cart track by Spittle Croft near Litton. This is also a bad weather alternative and joins the road to Dale Head. Follow the Pennine Way to Churn Milk Hole's deep depression on the left, then turn left and first right in about a kilometre to get to the bunkhouses of Dub Cote and then on to Horton.

Further Walking

Yorkshire Three Peaks Walk including Ingleborough, Whernside, Penyghent. Either enter the challenge event or do it yourself. Details of the event from Penyghent Stores, Horton-in-Ribblesdale, North Yorkshire BD24 0HE.

Whernside Cave and Fell Centre, Deepdale, the height point of 424m (1,391ft), the occupation road, High Nun House and return.

Sedbergh, Arant Haw, Calders, The Calf, Cautley Spout, Fawcett Bank and return.

Hawkswick, Arncliffe, Old Cote Little Moor, Moor End, Kettlewell, Knipe Scar and return (*see* map, page 94).

Chapter 10

WENSLEYDALE AND SWALEDALE WALKS

Under 'Further Walking' is an area which deserves a mention in its own right in any exploration of the Pennines and in particular of the Yorkshire Dales. Wensleydale and the accompanying River Ure, is a picturesque sprawling valley, much wider proportioned than Swaledale, perhaps slightly less intimate, yet containing innumerable walking possibilities. I have sited three walks which are representative of this dale's merits.

Maps   OS 1:50,000 series sheet No. 98. The 1:25,000 Leisure Series, Yorkshire Dales Northern and Central Area.
Transport   British Rail: Settle/Carlisle.
Accommodation   Wensleydale – Hawes Youth Hostel, Hawes, tel: 0969 667368 and Bainbridge Ings Campsite, Hawes, tel: 0969 667354. Swaledale – Keld Youth Hostel, Keld, tel: 0748 86259. Many guest houses, contact Yorkshire Dales National Park HQ, Grassington.

Wensleydale Walks

Hawes is a much visited market town situated on the Pennine Way, having a youth hostel, two good camping sites nearby, as well as bed and breakfast accommodation. It lies on crossroads, the main through route being east to west, but the north–south route between Swaledale and Ingleton is also well used. A good mountain road also goes south over to Langstrothdale to link Upper Wharfedale. Thus, Hawes is well placed. Plenty of buses come to Hawes. It has a National Park Information Centre utilizing the old station building, a museum of Wensleydale's past and a few decent pubs. Wensleydale cheese is manufactured in the town.

Without further ado, here are two walks using Hawes as a base.

Walk 1

Hawes, Bainbridge Ings, Burtersett, Cam High Road, circling Wether Fell and Drumaldrace, surely the easiest 600-metre (2,000-ft) mountain in the Yorkshire Dales! Join the original track to branch left down to Gayle and return to Hawes. It is a walk of excellent views.

Walk 2

Hawes, the Pennine Way north to Haylands Bridge, Sedbusk, High Clint, giving great retrospective views. Go over and down Low Clint, an easy limestone scar, to meet a track. Turn left or right, the left-hand route being quicker, to High Shaw. Take a lane signposted Fossdale, then steps to the thick woods surrounding the

Burtersett village, Wensleydale.

beck. There is a waterfall before you meet the road again which you soon leave turning right across enclosures to West House and into Hardraw. A 5-minute walk through private ground leads to England's highest single drop waterfall, Hardraw Force which is best seen in spate, plummeting over the craggy Scaur. A footbridge to the other bank overlooks the fall splendidly. Then return by walking the

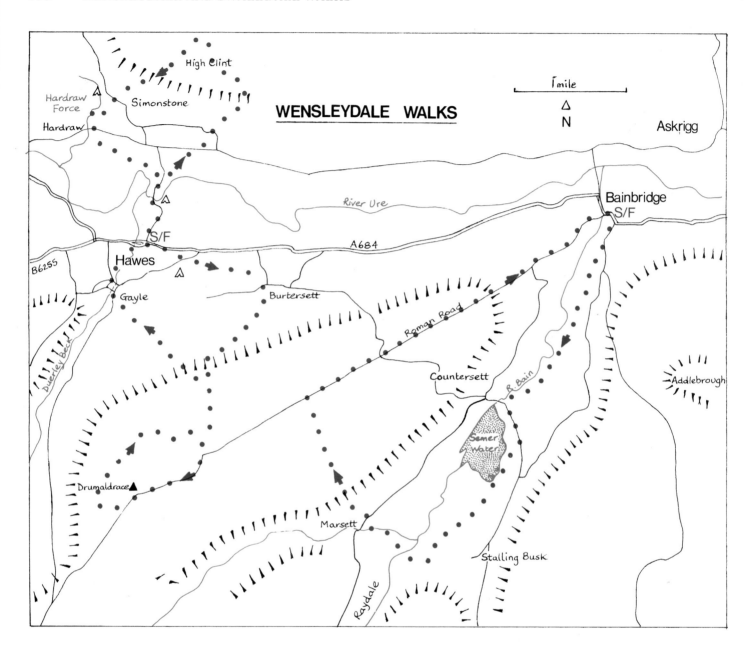

flagged stone path, (the Pennine Way) to Haylands Bridge and return to Hawes.

From Bainbridge, 6km (4 miles) down the dale from Hawes, a fine circuit can be made up Carpley Green Road, branching right over a knoll to reveal Semerwater serenely cradled ahead. The track descends to the River Bain to follow it by meadowland, then bear left to the road and continue around the shores of Semerwater, a natural lake of geological and botanical importance. Pass the tiny church of Stalling Busk which is sadly abandoned. Go via fields, and across a beck onto a track to Marsett which consists of a most pleasant collection of delightfully situated buildings. Go uphill via a track to level out near a scar edge and the Cam High Road which you follow almost all the way back to Bainbridge with views ahead of Wensleydale Fells most of the way.

After Hawes and Hardraw, the Pennine Way makes a very protracted ascent of the sprawling bulk of Great Shunner Fell.

The walking is more pleasant on either of the flanks than the peaty summit plateau and rather undistinguished top. However, even here, having patiently gone from one false shoulder to another, kidding the walker the summit is nigh when it is not, there is a sense of great isolation with many a square mile of moor and fell stretching in all directions, Wild Boar Fell

Hardraw Force (opposite). The highest single drop waterfall in England.

Semerwater, towards Marsett.

A mountain biker on Cam High Road, an ancient highway above Wensleydale.

Bainbridge, Wensleydale.

being about the most distinguished top on any nearer horizon. Clear weather certainly is the recipe for this huge fell, as in mist it can be drudgery to cross. Only in exceptionally clear conditions can the Cumbrian Mountains be seen. On the way down the eye will inevitably be drawn to the landscape of Upper Swaledale. Shunner has been conquered and now, many delights await the searching walker in the delectable Swaledale.

Swaledale Walks

Walk 1 Muker, Ivelet, Satron, Oxnop Gill, Crow Trees and return (*see* the Swaledale Walks map).

Field patterns near Hawes, Wensleydale.

Wensleydale, Hawes and Great Shunner Fell.

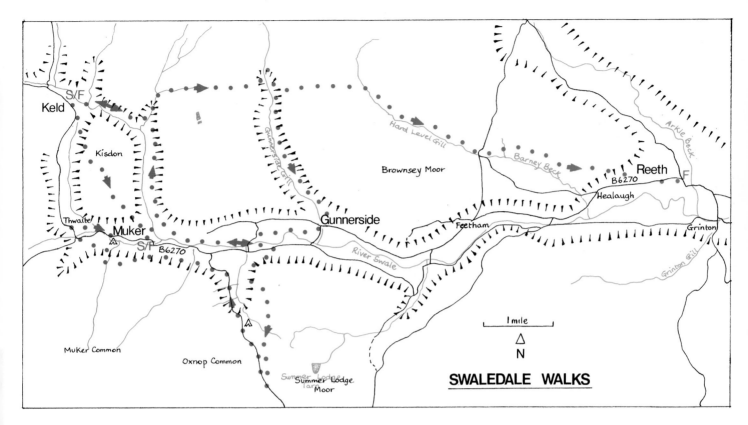

SWALEDALE WALKS

Muker. in its Swaledale setting.

From the delightfully situated Muker, pass behind the church through cottages to reach a meadow path which in summer is decked with flowers. Gap stiles lead to the bridge with lovely views upstream of the River Swale. Follow close to the river downstream near barns to Ivelet Bridge. Cross the bridge and turn left, following enclosures to Satron. Cross the B road to a walled track which leads uphill revealing views up and down dale. Falling away to the right is the declevity of Oxnop Beck cloaked in trees. Take a right turn to the thread buildings (which belong to Hill Top and Oxnop Ghyll farms). Descend the lane left to where it bends and steepens to find a path on the left. Be careful when picking your route across a deep cut beck. Then go more obviously on a general level above Muker, before descending a walled lane back to the village.

Walk 2 Keld, Kisdon, Muker, River Swale, Crackpot Hall and return (*see* the Swaledale Walks map).

Aigill, and its fields and barns seen in winter from Kisdon Hill.

Keld, North Yorkshire.

Leave Keld by the B6270. As the flanks of Kisdon loom up left, take a hard-core track into the dip and curve right, climbing the side of Kisdon. Note Angram and the walled enclosures are now below and to your right. Commence a fine crossing of Kisdon on fairly level ground. A grand view begins to open up over the upper dale and then you make a winding descent by the buildings of Kisdon to where Muker nestles below. Leave the village by the Walk 1 route, but having crossed the bridge go upstream, along the flat which is then followed by a gradual ascent, crossing the Swinner Gill at some spoils. Divert off track up to the right to look at Crackpot Hall then retrace your steps to go high above the wooded Swale gorge, skirting the trees that hug the hillside.

Looking upstream, River Swale near Muker.

Walls and barns, Kisdon, Swaledale.

Ahead, glimpse Keld before descending to the bridge over the Swale by waterfalls. Climb out on the right and return to Keld.

Walk 3 Muker, Swinnergill, East Grain, Gunnerside Gill, Gunnerside, Ivelet and return (*see* Swaledale Walks map).

Leave Muker as for Walk 1. Cross the bridge and head in the direction of Crackpot Hall. There are now two alternatives. One is to go to Crackpot Hall as in Walk 2, then picking up the thin track which skirts the steep sides of Swinnergill before going down to meet the beck at a bridge by a picturesque waterfall. The second alternative for scramblers is to keep the beck of Swinnergill on their left before going down to meet it. Best followed in low water, the gill forms a mini-gorge which is entered. Good sport can be had scrambling in the ever-narrowing upper reaches until emerging at the waterfall. Turn right up the East Grain to follow the Coast to Coast walk to the hushes of Gunnerside Gill. A super walk ensues by following the beck down on its east bank to reach Gunnerside. The pub may be welcome for the thirsty. A lovely return to Muker is made by walking along many field enclosures via gap stiles, with the River Swale never far away on the left – all in all a grand day's walking.

Chapter 11
TWO WALKS IN NIDDERDALE

Perhaps due to waterworks politics, Nidderdale was never included in the Yorkshire Dales National Park. Reasons other than this for its exclusion are perplexing, for Nidderdale is as fine a Yorkshire dale as any!

Maps	OS 1:50,000 No. 99 Northallerton and Ripon.
Transport	British Rail: Harrogate, West Yorkshire. The Road Car Company, tel: 0423 66061.
Accommodation	The TIC, Pateley Bridge (seasonal), tel: 0423 711147 and the TIC, Harrogate, Tel: 0423 525666.

Lofthouse, Stean, How Stean Gorge, Middlesmoor, Pott Moor, Lofthouse

Start out from the village of Lofthouse an original Viking settlement in a sheltered corner of upper Nidderdale, where the How Stean Beck meets the River Nidd. The village is quiet, almost echoey, the only disturbance being the distinct jingle of the village post office door as an occasional customer calls. Use the road to the How Stean Gorge, which crosses the beck. Then make a left turn towards Studfold Farm and its caravan site, but before reaching it, climb a steep unmetalled lane that passes a dwelling and barns, the second of which gives a green path to the right, follow this and go over walls and stiles via White Beck House. Pass another barn and go through a red gate into Stean which has a fine cluster of houses.

Across the valley is a good view of Middlesmoor, a classic hilltop village with a prominent church tower. From here a private way with permitted access is used to strike uphill on an ill-defined path where yellow arrows on a barn mark the route. The object beyond is to cross a deep valley full of trees. We personally found a narrow path alongside a fence above the

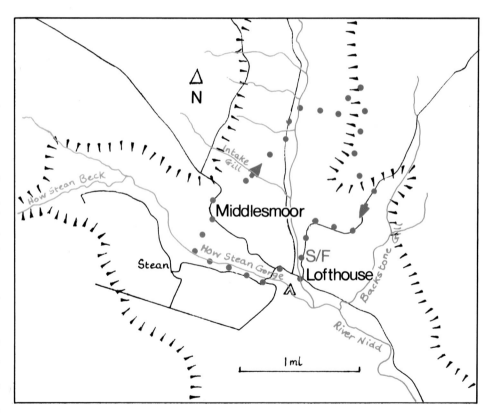

beck. This led to a waterworks bridge which can be climbed on to by a ladder. Another ladder just upstream on the other bank heralded a steep narrow path on to the moor which in turn led down by the abandoned dwelling of High Riggs. Then

an inhabited farm gave a good track down to a bridge in a wooded glade, where two becks meet by a waterfall tumbling over limestone. This is a fine spot for refreshment. Beyond this, it was necessary to keep tabs with the beck below. Undulations

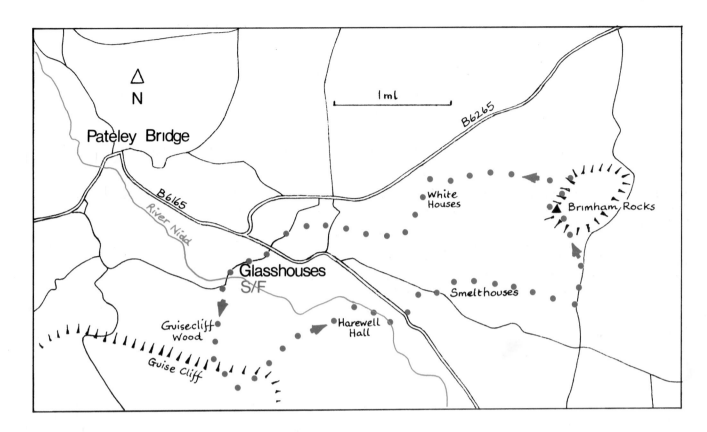

led us to the wooden bridge spanning the gorge, now narrow and funnelling water through. The bridge was merely a viewpoint, and turning back, we climbed the green hill to the road which bent round steeply right at 1:4, to the village of Middlesmoor.

The above route, despite being shown as rights of way on the map is not easily followed, however, it is worth it if you manage to do so. The alternative would be to walk by the signposted lane to How Stean Gorge, enter the private pathway along the gorge to eventually cross the wooden bridge and climb to Middlesmoor. This is considerably shorter.

Hilltop villages are rare, so a visit to Middlesmoor on a pleasant day is a must. It is a higgledy-piggledy place, with the Crown Inn sat back high on a platform above the minor through road which bisects the village. Off right, a worn cobbled path twists round cottages to reach the stout church of St Chad with many gravestones in the two-tiered cemetery.

By the church wall is the following inscription on a gravestone:

'Ye who in life's fair morning see the grassy turf which covers us.
Here gathered in a good old age: Let God your earliest thoughts engage.
Remember Him in days of youth, and swerve not from the paths of truth:
Then like a shock of ripened grain, fresh reaped in, Autumn from the plain.
Death will your weary frame convey to slumber on its parent clay:
While free from your every earthly leaven, Angels will bear your soul to heaven.'

I'm going to burst into tears! Seriously, though it is a befitting piece of prose, particularly as you gaze from a bench on the upper tier of the cemetery to the fine study of Nidderdale below with the Gouthwaite Reservoir prominent.

Leaving Middlesmoor, find a way on to a walled lane to the east aspect of the

Upper How Stean Gorge near Lofthouse.

Middlesmoor, a hilltop village in Upper Nidderdale.

Upper Nidderdale in autumn.

church which leads to a beautiful descent into Upper Nidderdale and the road to Scar House Reservoir. On the skyline ahead is a curious tower. It is a stiff haul up to this by way of Thrope House, a proud farm dwelling. Turn upwards by a barn to a conifer wood on a twisting green path then go through lovely silver birches to views of the upper dale beyond. The squat tower is a purpose-built shooting lodge which has the blue letter R inside a white circle on three of its faces. This stands for Ramsden, the owner of the Middlesmoor estate. Follow the track along the moor edge which turns left and, through a gate on the right, will lead easily to the road, with the eye being drawn towards Gouthwaite Reservoir. An easy descent gives first, views of Middlesmoor, then Lofthouse, your point of return.

Pateley Bridge, Gouthwaite Reservoir, and Upper Nidderdale from Guisecliff.

Glasshouses, Guisecliff, Smelthouses, Brimham Moor/Rocks, Whitehouses, and Return

This is a varied outing with pleasing scenery all the way, using the same maps as for Walk 1. It has two superb places of interest and much in between as a circular walk based on Glasshouses. The object is to get up to Yorke's Folly, a tower on the skyline of Guisecliff, reputed to have been built by the Yorke family of Bewerley just because there was a need for labour at the time! The tower can be reached through a path which strikes off right in the first patch of woodland out of Glasshouses. It reaches an unmetalled road and joins a surfaced one which climbs to the plateau and bears leftwards, to find its way along the edge of Guisecliff whilst aiming for the prominent mast. The cliffs are a tremendous vantage point over much of Nidderdale, with Glasshouses prominent below, Brimham Rocks far across the dale, and views along the dale all the way beyond Pateley Bridge to Gouthwaite Reservoir and Middlesmoor.

Another way up Guisecliff goes on a westward trending path through woods predominently of birch, which are perhaps best encountered in autumn foliage. From the mast, which on this alternative is just a point of height to aim for, it is necessary to descend immediately on a steep green path, then go through an iron gate, and make for the edge of a conifer plantation. Keep left of the wall and the plantation and amble down fields to Harewell Hall, a working cattle farm, then cross the River Nidd by a wooden bridge. The river bank is followed for several hundred metres before a beck bars the way. A small footbridge gives an arrow-marked path to Low Laithe (Knox Hall). Go straight across the B6165, down a lane that goes by a restaurant and a wooded beck to emerge on the narrow lane to Smelthouses.

Eagle and Castle Rocks, Brimham, Nidderdale.

Glasshouses from Guisecliff.

Idol Rock, Brimham (note the 45-cm/18-in pedestal)!

The name is taken from the lead smelting mill established there in the fourteenth century by monks from Fountains Abbey. The narrow road you take on the right makes it hard to believe that it was once the original turnpike road to Knaresborough. Turn left by the next house up a walled lane, then go right on a bridleway which gradually ascends through scattered woodland to the road on Brimham Moor.

What follows as you enter the car park at Brimham Rocks is a landscape that is a connoisseurs' delight. Brimham Rocks is an eastern outpost of the Pennines, it is outstanding and unique in character with weird rocks of every conceivable shape and size decorated around their bases by a tree, fern, heather and bilberry garden. Every twisted layer, hole, pedestal, pinnacle, fissure, cranny, chimney, wall, groove and buttress under the sun seems to be in its collection. A glacier of the last ice age laid bare thick layers of gritstone which have been subjected to weather erosion ever since. The rocks come in individual separated collections and are christened with such animal names as 'Dancing Bear', 'Elephant Rock', 'Hippopotamus Head' and 'Dog's Head'. Idol Rock is 5m (15ft) tall, weighs 180 tonnes (180 tons) and is supported by a ludicrous 46-cm (18-in) pedestal, but it has defied gravity so far! I'd hate to be the guy who walks by when it collapses. Instant fossilized man!

Leave these sculptures by a track going on to a hardcore road, whereupon a sharp left turn leads to buildings where glass is engraved. Carry on downhill, through gates, cross over the beck which feeds Mill House by a footbridge, then continue upwards again where the path runs beside a detached house. Turn left towards White Houses where the route is on a level grassy track beyond a 'Please Shut the Gate' sign. This track becomes walled beneath some small gritstone outcrops. Turn up and loop round to the Raikes, then go downhill to cross the main road into Glasshouses.

There are many feasible walks in Nidderdale since its reaches are long and widespread, but I feel the two chosen are classical samples of this fine dale, worth any walker's weekend.

Chapter 12

THE MALLERSTANG HORSESHOE WALK

Peter Denby, an equipment outfitter of Kirkby Stephen and Richard Sewell designed this walk whose full title adds the 'Nine Standards Yomp'. It has become an annual challenge event on the first Sunday in June. With assistance, or without, the walk is possible at any time. This is a very worthwhile corner of the Pennines, where the National Park meets fells curiously outside its borders and is of no less character for that, completing a 37km (23 miles) circuit.

Maps	OS sheet Nos. 91 and 98.
Transport	Rail Services: Settle/Carlisle Station at Kirkby Stephen. *See* other notes in this book giving rail details or ring any major British Rail station.
	Bus Services: Primrose Coaches, tel: 091 325567. OK Travel, tel: 0388 604581 and Scottish City Link, tel: 031 537 5717.
Accommodation	There is a youth hostel at Kirkby Stephen, tel: 07683 71793. For others tel: Tourist Information Centre at Kirkby Stephen, 07683 71199.

The start and finish is at Kirkby Stephen.

Note: There is a booklet or further detailed information on this walk available from Peter Denby, tel: 0930 71671.

The Mallerstang Valley is a simple north-south divide splitting fells of the north-western Yorkshire Dales from those, including Wild Boar Fell, outside the National Park. It is quite long, housing the B6259, the Settle/Carlisle railway (which has been reprieved), and the young River Eden which is the cause of its present-day shape. The aim is to circuit the two sides of the valley, based on Kirkby Stephen return. The route first leaves the town from the A685 to head for the historic Wharton Hall, clearly viewing its fifteenth-century gatehouse when passing between the modern farm buildings. Cross over the Settle/Carlisle railway line by a bridge, then hug the line on 'Tommy Road'. Next, ascend Wharton Fell and its solitary field house and the track ends by old stone workings at Greenlaw Rigg. On gaining the summit of Little Fell, there is a rewarding view to the Mallerstang and Eden Valleys. A small descent is followed by a punishing and steep climb to meet an ancient drovers road out of the dale below.

The outlook is wild now as the job of

Pendragon Castle stands guard at the end of the Mallerstang Valley with the Nab of Wild Boar Fell behind.

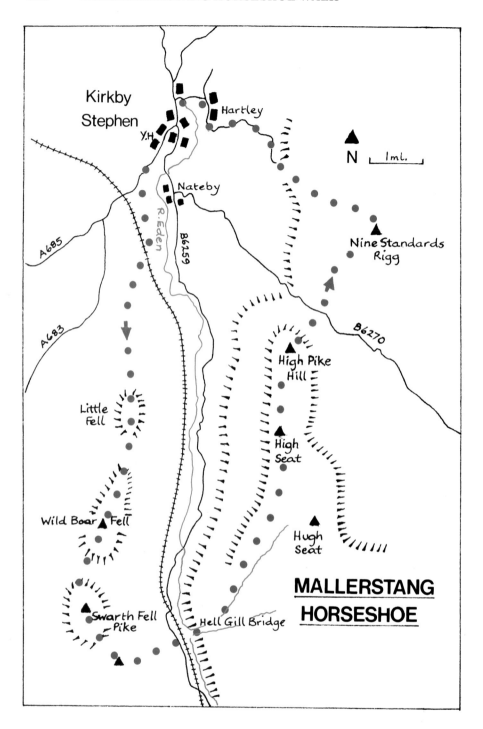

climbing Wild Boar Fell is undertaken. Note the steep scarp slope of The Nab, which is really a promontory at the end of the flat top of the plateau of Wild Boar Fell. Although tempted to follow the edge of the rim, the walker should have enough will-power to visit the trig point on Wild Boar Fell to gaze, particularly at the Howgills. Elsewhere, the rim has a number of cairns on the Nab, which provide bird's-eye views into the dale below. You are then well able to perceive the more mountainous forms of this fine fell, which are only prevalent on its east side as its

The Nab forms a steep spur from Wild Boar Fell.

Aisgill Moor Cottages and Wild Boar Fell.

western extremities tail away into featureless moorland.

From the trig point, you soon descend to a saddle which cradles a small tarn, and this will no doubt catch the eye in clear conditions. A wall is then followed to a wire fence and thus onward to Swarth Fell Pike, with this route also giving views south towards Ingleborough and Whernside in clear conditions. The path loops round off this top to descend to Aisgill Moor Cottages where Wild Boar Fell presents a craggy scarp and bold-edged sweep into the valley.

From this point the route has, in a manner of speaking, turned the corner. Hell Gill's Force, a substantial waterfall, plummets in a clear sweep over an amphitheatre to rush away in a deep gorge below the road. Cross over the superb stone-arched Hell Gill Bridge above a limestone gorge, aiming upwards over an open fell to gain Hangingstone Scar which should be well etched out in good weather. Steadier going leads to High Seat, at 709m (2,326ft), the highest point of the walk. There now follows a wild moorland stretch with a gradual descent to High Pike Hill with good vistas in virtually every direction. High Pike Hill suddenly presents a drop, where beyond, Nine Standards Rigg and its cairns are the skyline. To reach this, descend to the B6270, Nateby–Keld Road, beyond which are limestone pavements. At this point a stretch of peat hags materializes, which are either crossed or can be avoided by walking round to the north, an area which is shown as Rollinson Haggs on the OS map. The well-marked coast to coast path is joined, leading to the trig point on Nine Standards Rigg.

The Nine Standards are a few hundred metres to the north. Fans of the Royal Family have erected a direction indicator to commemorate the wedding of Prince Charles and Lady Diana Spencer, on 29 July 1981.

From the Nine Standards it is necessary to locate Faraday Gill with its ruined shelter and a stone cairn. Cross the beck and keep to a stone wall to meet the metalled lane that descends to Hartley, whose beck

Hell Gill Force (opposite) the first major feature of the young River Eden.

View north-east from High Pike Hill towards Nine Standards Rigg.

is crossed by a stone footbridge. Halfway down the village, turn left at a lane, which then leads to a path that meets the River Eden. This provides a pleasant riverside interlude before crossing Frank's Bridge and entering Kirkby Stephen.

Further Walking

Wild Boar Fell can be ascended from Hazelgill (GR 779998). This route goes up open pastureland, then through some limestone clints and up a steep scarp to join the main ridge to the Nab. Follow the route to Aisgill Moor Cottages and then use the old High Way which runs pleasantly through the valley, following a stone wall along much of its lower length to meet the B6259 just south of the start.

From Kirkby Stephen, follow lanes and weeded paths upstream on the River Eden to a spectacular gorge at Coop

Wild Boar Fell from High Pike Hill in Winter.

for the Pennine Way, there are very few rights of way and dominant scenery to tempt even the most searching of walkers, though I keep looking at the path shown which enables an east to west (or vice versa) route between Baldersdale and Brough. One feature of interest might be God's Bridge, a natural limestone bridge which is very accessible from the A66 if you are not doing the Pennine Way. Baldersdale is wild and often windswept with only the reservoirs holding some attention, and Low Birk Hat, the former house of the well-known Hannah Hauxwell who lived a Spartan life there for 60 years before moving to more comfort in nearby Cotherstone.

Karnal Hole and back. This is a simple worthwhile excursion.

Northwards from the Tan Hill Inn to Teesdale, the Pennines present a vast wilderness of almost level moorland, with the only disturbances being the traffic arteries of the A66 and B6276 roads. Save

Chapter 13

THE NORTH PENNINES CIRCUIT

This is an isolated walk in wild rolling fells in England's last 'wilderness'. Except for the Pennine Way section, walking in this region has been little documented. Careful pre-planning gives a circular walk based on Middleton-in-Teesdale which first follows the Pennine Way. This is a classic section and well worth a repeat. Better still, if you walk the Pennine Way from north to south as we did, so as to see this stretch in a different light. Except for Alston, Allendale Town and Stanhope, services are sparse, but the route is logically connected to accommodation stops with reasonable distances for fit walkers in between. The toughest day is the traverse of Cross Fell between Dufton and Alston. Beyond Alston, paths are sometimes little trodden and care is required to locate and follow them.

Maps	OS Teesdale 1:25,000 Outdoor Leisure series. The 1:25,000 Pathfinder series, Alston, No NY 64/74 and Allenheads and Rookhope, No. 84/94 of the 1:50,000 series. Map Nos. 87, 91 and 92 of the 1:25,000 series are also recommended.
Transport	Rail Services: There are none anywhere near! Darlington is about 48km (30 miles) away.
	Bus Services: United 76/A and X76 can be used, connecting with BR at Darlington, tel: 0325 468771.
Accommodation	There are guest houses in Middleton-in-Teesdale as well as Langdon Beck Youth Hostel, tel: 0833 22228; Dufton Youth Hostel, tel: 07683 51236; Allendale, 'The Tea Rooms,' tel: 0434683 575; and Rookhope Inn, tel: 0388 517215.
	You start and finish at Middleton-in-Teesdale.

Day 1 Half day to reach Middleton. Walk from Middleton to Langdon Beck: Day 2 Langdon Beck to Dufton: Day 3 Dufton to Alston: Day 4 Alston to Allendale Town: Day 5 Allendale Town to Rookhope: Day 6 Rookhope to Middleton (return).

A North Pennines Circuit

Day 1

From wherever you live, use this day to reach Middleton-in-Teesdale. It takes half a day or less to walk from Middleton to Langdon Beck Youth Hostel. The Pennine Way has been written about so much, yet I beg to offer some more details on this worthy section.

The Pennine Way along the River Tees provides about the wildest, most beautiful river walk anywhere in England. The river trundles down from the vast swell of the

Middleton-in-Teesdale from Ramsgill, Kirkcarrion.

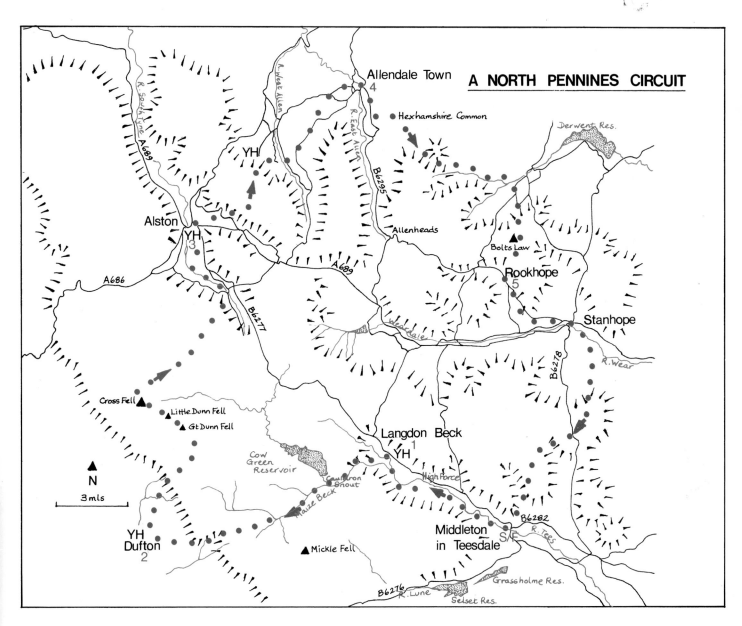

A NORTH PENNINES CIRCUIT

Milburn Forest moorland watershed creating three classic waterfalls along its path, two of which are passed between Middleton and Langdon Beck. To reach these, begin quite serenely by joining the river path on its south bank via a bridge on the B6276 going south out of town.

This walk is never far from the river. It starts as a cart track then becomes a thin path crossing a stile designer's paradise with tree-lined river banks most of the way and meadowland decked with flowers in spring and summer. Note Holwick Scar

on the left, and proceed to Scoberry Bridge where the river takes on a rougher bed, as rocks begin to split its flow. There are flowers on top of these rocks, braving the cracks. The river bank opposite is sylvan, as it leads to Low Force which is picturesque and colourful, particularly in spate against an autumn backcloth. The next objective, High Force, the largest English waterfall (but not the highest) can be heard as you approach through a juniper grove. The roar gets louder until the eye is riveted by the actual scene. It is

savage, yet beautiful as the water thunders through the gap and over a 20-metre (70-foot) precipice into its amphitheatre of dolerite cliffs. Rich vegetation dares to encase the surroundings which are more spectacular on this side of the river than from the frequented hotel path on the opposite bank.

A section of calmer river is interrupted by the ugly Dine Holme Quarry. Even the classic Upper Tees has not escaped unblemished. Climbing up to Bracken Rigg, make a diversion to the edge of the hill to

note the superb S-bend on the Tees below the junipers. It snakes towards the scattered whitewashed dwellings of Forest in Teesdale that typify these parts of County Durham. Reach the rocky outcrops of High Crag and glance ahead to the edge of Cronkley Scar. Go down the bouldery path and up a field to a gate by the corner shed of Cronkley Farm. Then go down to a river bridge and along the river path until you reach a farm drive that leads right, to climb slightly to the B6277 and Langdon Beck Youth Hostel.

This part of Teesdale which you have passed through is unworthy of just one visit. Return if you can, perhaps in the guise of a naturalist or botanist, a photographer or artist, or simply to be at one with creation there.

Low Force, River Tees.

High Force, River Tees (England's largest waterfall).

S-bend on the River Tees towards Forest in Teesdale.

Falcon Clints, Upper Tees.

Day 2

This is a journey into wild remote country starting with entry into the Upper Teesdale National Nature Reserve, whose sign is encountered on the Pennine Way path. The grass is traversed towards the gap in the hills where the Tees flows. The fresh smell of open country lures the walker into this lonely moorland stronghold bisected by the Maize Beck and its tributaries. Pass the white farm building and look at Cronkley Scar to the left, on the opposite side of the river. Continue walking on a wide grass strath, until a boulder field has to be traversed, interspersed by duckboards. The main watercourse disappears rightwards around the corner formed by Falcon Clints, then suddenly, Cauldron

Cauldron Snout in spate, Upper Teesdale.

Birkdale, one of the most isolated farms in England.

Snout forces its way through an upstanding fortress of dolerite.

I do not wish rain on anyone, but after it, The Snout is a raging force to be seen at its best. Ascend its right edge, scrambling if you wish, to cross the Cow Green Reservoir outlet and head for Birkdale which is one of the most isolated of farmhouses in England. From here, the moorland is wild and bleak with Mickle Fell sprawling to the South. And the next few kilometres can be boggy and tedious after what has gone before. In bad weather, it is better to follow the Maize Beck all the way to the wooden bridge, passing little rocky intrusions. In dry conditions, it may be possible to potter along the low stream bed on the square slabs of limestone. Approaching the bridge when the stream is low, carefully walk up the mini-gorge of limestone runnels, or keep to the bank above if you are feeling less adventurous. After the double back across the limestone clints, another spectacle awaits in the form of High Cup Nick, or just High Cup (as the nick is just one cleft in the rocks). Ahead is a semi-circular rim which falls away into a valley more akin to a canyon, this in turn is rimmed by a level tier of basalt crags. Look carefully for a pillar of basalt near the cliff edge called 'Nichols' Chair'. From near this airy perch, gaze far below to the stream bed as it wiggles through the valley floor, at the same time leading the eye to the flat verdant Eden Valley, beyond which the Lakeland mountains may be seen. The path which is sometimes rocky, meanders over the

Bridge over Upper Maize Beck, Pennine Way, Tees Watershed.

High Cup Nick and Narrowgate Beacon.

High Cup Nick and the basalt rim.

Dufton Village and Dufton Pike.

shoulder. Take one more look at the canyon with Middle Tongue being the hill across the void, then proceed pleasantly downhill to the fine village of Dufton.

The eyes of hill lovers will surely be drawn to the shapely crest of Dufton Pike behind the village, whilst the village houses are arranged neatly around an elongated village green which is bedecked by trees. The youth hostel is very well appointed and serves good meals.

Day 3

There are many mountains whose summits are more accessible than Cross Fell. There are also many towns whose descents are nearer from summits than Alston is from Cross Fell. So, the order of the day is an early start because the distance is long and the walk is strenuous. Start easy enough by a lane to Coatsike on the sharp road bend west of Dufton. Dufton Pike ahead dominates, and as you climb, notice how Murton Fell echoes

Dufton Pike's shape. Passing Coatsike, the path keeps right of an overgrown lane to Halsteads, then crosses a clapper bridge over Great Rundale Beck. The climb is lengthy, but when there is good weather, it is compensated by the views over the Eden Valley. Note that in bad conditions it is advisable to take the metalled lane out of Knock village all the way up to Great Dun Fell. Why bother with the purist's way in poor conditions? (As I duck the flak from the purists!)

Otherwise, the moor is crossed passing a number of cairns in a seemingly endless climb to reach the large cairn of Knock Old Man and further cairns scattered over Knock Fell. At last, it is an easy stride to the radar station on Great Dun Fell, where, if the wind is blowing, which it usually does, the masts howl in eerie vibration. The experience, particularly under misty conditions, reminds me of an abandoned moonbase. Perhaps this is the kindest description!

Follow the undulations traversing Little

Cross Fell from the Vale of Eden.

The author at the large beacon on Cross Fell.

Dunn Fell and climb steadily to the rim of Cross Fell. To the north and east, vast tracts of Pennine uplands sweep away, a seemingly empty wilderness. To the south and west, there is the patchwork of the Eden Valley environs. A large beacon cairn, 3m (10ft) tall, heralds the plateau of Cross Fell, which is so flat and expansive that several football pitches could be accommodated here. But who'd come and watch the games? The spectators would have to be paid to come up here!

It can be difficult to locate the trig point because it is often capped in cloud, however, this is now backed by a cross-shaped wall shelter, so you can pick your spot out of the wind. I wish you good clear conditions, because this, much more than the terrain makes the traverse worthwhile.

Descend for a kilometre or so, first down the scree and boulder edge, then on an often splashy slope where springs begin to feed the vast drainage system of the Tyne and Eden. Turn right at a large cairn, passing a hut on the right, and then

From Little Dun Fell to Great Dun Fell with Mickle Fell and Cow Green Reservoir on the horizon.

embark on a protracted descent on a good trail, crossing in places, the remains of old lead mines and fragments of fluorspar, a mauve or purple rock crystal. The trail is the old corpse road from Kirkland to Garrigill, and eventually after spending quite a time and distance on it above the 450-metre (1,500-foot) contour, the Way leads down a walled lane and winds up in Garrigill. This is a serene village having a tree-decked green. Refreshments and accommodation are possible here, but Alston lies ahead.

From Garrigill, follow the south bank of the River South Tyne until a fine footbridge to the north side gives a tree-lined route, leading to open enclosures, and on to Alston.

The modern, comfortable youth hostel is situated alongside the route, just before the main road is reached. Alston, though in Cumbria, owes much more allegiance to Northumberland to which it is geographically and socially allied. The main road uphill through the town is still cobbled and supports a fine market cross-shelter. On either side of the road are the buildings of Six Fathom Hazzle, the local sandstone. Many moons ago, when my wife and I reached Alston doing the Pennine Way from north to south, she was in desperate need of another pair of walking boots. The only shop selling these items was closed, its owner had died the week before! She did not get relief from her boots for another five days until we reached Hawes!

Day 4

Vacate Alston on the twisting lane just by the Turks Head public house with the steepled church left. Ignore a sharp left on the lane to head straight for the River Nent. Cross this and follow a walled path which climbs diagonally across walled fields to the whitewashed Corby Gates Farm, then go across more walled enclosures to a metalled lane. The objective is to reach Allendale Town, and there seems to be much high moorland barring the way. Therefore, progress to a narrow metalled lane which strikes uphill, turning sharp left towards the old lead mines off the B6294. As this is ascended, look back down the valley to the walled patterns

Alston, an important market town in the North Pennines.

Retrospect of Alston area and the surrounding fells from near Blagill.

West Allendale, a serene North Pennines Valley.

near Corby Gates Farm and your last glimpse of Alston.

There is fragmented evidence of old lead mining spoils as the lane, just about metalled, reaches a T-junction, where on the right a well-surfaced road ends. Take the left walled stony lane up onto the bleak moorland, and be careful in mist where it peters out. In these conditions, a north-easterly bearing will be needed to descend steadily to the well-defined runnel of Well-hope Burn. The lead in to this is the corner of a long wall. Keep this about 100 metres on the right, and proceed parallel to it so that you continue on a north-easterly bearing to old mine workings.

In good weather note the fine aspect of moorland spurs and lower farms leading into West Allendale. Cross the Mohope

A retrospect of West Allendale from Point 494m on the road.

and Wellhope Burns by two footbridges to the farm of Hesleywell, then carry on to 'The Middle', a private house, and over the shoulder to Broadlea. The road goes for 250 metres up to a gate and then continues diagonally down to a footbridge over the River West Allen. It keeps below the trees until it reaches a wicket gate, then swings right zigzagging steeply to Greenleyclough. Turn right along the road to the signed drive of Taylorburn, then take a steep green path which arrives on the Nenthead/Allendale road near a height point of 494m (1,621ft) on the OS map. (1:50,000 series). Pause here to look back across the wild vistas of West Allendale, then go easily along the high road for 2 kilometres.

On the left you will see a wooden gate and signpost stating 'Carriers Way' which leads to two forlorn chimney landmarks on the wide moor. These were smelt chimneys for lead mining. The true path swings round left to miss the second, more intact chimney. It is possible to follow the old flue with care. Either choice leads to Fell House from which the metalled lane joins a road on the right, to descend into Allendale Town. From the moor, extensive views are possible to the north as far as the Cheviots, and Allendale Town can be seen as your objective. The town lies on a plateau above the twisting River East Allen which is very sylvan hereabouts. Stout Georgian or Victorian buildings encircle a central block which includes

'The Tea Rooms' and a post office. Allendale Town mainly grew through lead mining and is distinctly northern in character. A seasoned map reader, Allendale Town always seeks to confuse me with its several roads radiating from its nucleus. Accommodation is plentiful here, though I recommend 'The Tea Rooms'.

Day 5

You may have to think carefully (like I do about orientation in Allendale Town), but if you are correct, you will have left it on a lane which double bends uphill to level out with good panoramas of Dryburn Moor and Acton Moor. Catton and its mast are easily seen behind. You vacate the lane by a walled road on the left. This leads to the open Westburnhope Moor. This is followed by a wild, yet pretty crossing of this

Smelt chimney remains, Dryburn Moor near Allendale Town.

South of Allendale town, looking at Catton and the Mast.

bracken and heather moor and there is one feature to aim for, Rowantree Clough, a shaly cutting from which springs Stobbylee Burn. Above this to the left, the way leads towards the isolated farm of Harwood Shield When we trod this route, there was an old railway waggon just before the farm in which we took elevenses.

Turn right and cross the burn on a bridge utilizing a good farm track over a hill brow towards a plantation. Join a path on the left, then go by the old dwelling of Riddlehamhope. Scenic panoramas open up on a well-defined forestry track. They give views of the valley enclosing the Beldon Burn. A kilometre of very pretty walking which flirts with the conifer plantations, brings you to a right turn by a

Westburnhope Moor, a wild crossing beyond Allendale.

Beldon Side, a semi-forested valley towards Hunstanton.

On Bolts Law, giving extensive views north.

corner of a small plantation. This goes downhill to enter the woods enclosing the Beldon Burn, and crosses a footbridge into County Durham. Follow the river upstream via a meadow to U-turn back into the firs. Head upwards where you reach open daylight toward the solitary church at Hunstanworth. It is necessary to road walk past a collection of dwellings called Townfield and up to the mining area of Ramshaw. This is an industrial waste-land, a contrast to the day's journey so far.

The exit from this place is hard to find, but you'll know your route is about right if you see a chimney poking out of a dip about half a kilometre to the left. The path is indistinct, but your eyes should locate the lump of Bolts Law ahead and to the right. Behind and to the left, it may be possible to see the Cheviots and parts of Tyneside etched out by high-rise blocks. The heathery way skirts the swell of Bolts Law to descend gently to a sheepfold and then joins a broad green line of a dismantled

railway. Follow this down the Boltslaw Incline with fine views over Upper Wear-dale's rolling fells. Suddenly the gradient steepens and the village of Rookhope is entered. Accommodation can be found at the Rookhope Inn.

Day 6

There are two choices open to the walker leaving Rookhope. Neither one super-cedes the other in terms of validity, but

Rookhope, County Durham.

the one over the lane and paths high above the Rookhope Burn gives excellent views into Weardale and down to Stanhope as it descends. On the southern end of Rookhope, the roads divide, so bear left and go for about two kilometres then make a right turn into the drive of Ambling Gate. Contour the hillside to Burnt Walls and Ashy Bank. Do not lose height, but in fact gain it slightly as you pass a larger farm and proceed along the broader swell which is parallel to the lane above. This means you go via West Bewdley, a Worcestershire name in County Durham! At a good drive, descend to Guys Close, go through it, and then turn left to meet the A689, in order to walk if required into Stanhope. You will not have failed to notice the domineering chimney stack of the Blue Circle Cement Works down in Weardale near Eastgate. I'm just glad it's not in Teesdale, as it is a bad enough intrusion on the landscape here! However, it provides work for the surrounding populace.

The alternative route out of Rookhope is for stream and river walking enthusiasts. Either take the old railway line to Smailsburn, or walk the minor road to a footbridge over the Rookhope Burn. The path is sometimes indistinct and spongy as it keeps near the line of the wooded burn to Hole House, where it becomes an enclosed lane going straight into Eastgate. Take the A689 left, then first right on a lane which goes over the River Wear at a twin-arched bridge. There is a public footpath to the left, which is really the drive into Hagbridge Caravan Park. There is also a builder's yard and a railway on the left, a mineral line from the cement works. The drive snakes into the caravan park which is pleasantly sited in a birch and pine copse on the river bank. The path follows the River Wear until it strikes the B6278 looping over the river. I was amazed and disheartened by the visual waste material almost continuously littering each side of the river all the way to the B-road. This is the Weardale Way, and is not a good advert for the route!

River Wear near Stanhope.

Above Stanhope.

Stanhope could be visited to stock up with iron rations as there is wild walking all the way to Middleton-in-Teesdale.

Continue on the Weardale Way on the south side of the river to join the Heather View Caravan Park and the lane from Shittlehope. Opposite a neat group of terraced houses, take the public footpath through a gap stile. Although the map shows quarry works, the spoils are now grassed over, so approach them via the Cow Burn and ascend to a prominent ruin. Cross the unmetalled quarry road through a gate, then shortly turn right through a white gate to plod upwards with the dilapidated farm of Peat Side a useful landmark. Go over this green hillside to traverse the

shoulder of Catterick Moss and a rougher moor, where a fine green path descends giving good aspects of the Bollihope Burn, a favourite haunt of Sunday drivers. Notice the curious spoil heaps alongside the burn, easily seen from above. Follow the burn left to the minor road, emerging on to it behind a small plantation. Walk up the road now, to take the V-cut in the Howden Burn which is on the left at the end of the road railings.

Ahead is a wild moorland crossing with only the B6278 linking civilization. The idea is to cross this road and head for the disused mine (grid reference 977307) and the Great Eggleshope Beck. In bad weather the indistinct start to the track

across the road may be difficult to find. Therefore, take the road over the pass to a track on the right with a moorland reservoir as the landmark. This leads over heather to the above burn.

Great Eggleshope Beck is a sheltered watercourse with three disused, but sturdy mining buildings reached by a ford on a good track, or a narrow plank footbridge adjacent to this. Up on the skyline on the right, is a used shooting cabin. Paths at the mine buildings are confusing and do not seem to go where you would think they should. Some metres up beyond these buildings is a gate in a wall. Go via this and a square hummock on the nearest skyline. This tedious ascent levels out on another heathery moor. Keep aiming for the highest point on Monks Moor until the long downhill begins opening up excellent views of Teesdale. Emerge on the bend in the minor road and walk its last couple of kilometres to Middleton-in-Teesdale to complete this North Pennines Circuit.

Further Walking in North Pennines

High Force Hotel, Ettersgill, Hanging Shaw, Hodge Hall, Sayer Hill, Pennine Way and return. At first, this walk is elevated above the wide sweeps of Teesdale, giving excellent views and contact with attractive whitewashed Teesdale farms. The walk then turns to meet the

Mine buildings, Great Eggleshope Beck.

Teesdale farms near Langdon Beck.

Pennine Way in order to follow its superb section back to High Force.

Hilton, Hilton Fell (when red flag is not flying!), Maize Beck, High Cup Nick, Dufton and return. It may pay to have a car left in Dufton to avoid the protracted walk back to Hilton village.

Kirkland, Cross Fell, Great Dun Fell, Milburn, Wythwaite and return. However there is a shorter route by descending Wildboar Scar.

North of Alston, apart from the North Pennines Circuit, the Pennine Way continues to the Roman Wall. At first it may be found pernikcety as it avoids road walking by circuitous wanderings – one, which if taken will include three sides of a seemingly unnecessary square to pursue its way north. This is often avoided by an unofficial straight line across fields between Harbut Law and Gilderdale Burn. Beyond Lintley Farm, it takes on the pretty riverside of the South Tyne, only to leave it much too soon to walk via a multitude of stiles eventually crossing heather and bracken following the Roman Maiden Way. North of Lambley Colliery the Way is a necessary bore. The real Pennine hills are about to end at the Carlisle/Newcastle gap, but plod on in order to reach a befitting finale in Hadrian's Wall Country. However, I am sure that Pennine Way walkers will see their official route to the very end in Kirk Yetholm; but for the Pennines proper, and the purposes of this book I shall end these explorations at Hadrian's Wall.

Chapter 14
A HADRIAN'S WALL CIRCUIT

The Pennines have nearly petered out in this part of the world, but if you enliken the shape of the Pennines to a billowy ocean then Hadrian's Wall country is like the lines of surf from that ocean as seen rippling into some bay. The terrain is exposed and windswept, the dales are shallow and several concurrent ridges from 30–100m (100–300ft) high make parallel lines from east to west. They are like waves, gentle slopes on their south side and abrupt ones, even cliffs on their north flanks. Several lakes or loughs are trapped at the base of north-facing sills of dolerite. Along the most continuous and generally highest of these ridges runs Hadrian's Wall.

Maps	The 1:50,000 series No. 87, Hexham, Haltwhistle and surrounding area.
Transport	Rail Services: Run from Newcastle and Carlisle, stopping at Barden Mill.
	Bus Services: National Express Coaches from Newcastle and Carlisle, Northumbria Bus Service No. 685.
Accommodation	There are guest houses at Hexham, Haltwhistle and Barden Mill or you can stay at the Once Brewed Youth Hostel.

I recommend the 'Hadrian's Wall Country' booklet by Tynedale Council available at Hexham and other places.

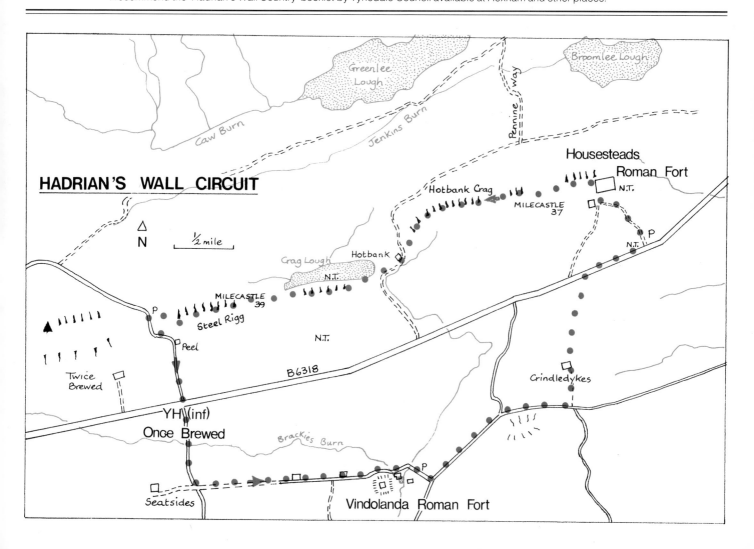

Vindolanda Roman Fort showing the quarters.

From accommodation at Hexham, Halt-whistle and Barden Mill, or the Once Brewed Youth Hostel, there is a stimulating 13-km (8-mile) walk starting from the visitor centre car park adjacent to the youth hostel. The hostel warden suggests following the wall first, but I suggest it is better as a finale. Therefore, it is down the lane southwards from the hostel and turn left at the sign for Vindolanda Roman Fort. The long straight lane follows the line of an old Roman road and soon, it is

possible to enter the Roman fort by a gate house and for an ample charge.

It is not my scene to visit ruins and think of what might have been. In fact, I find them depressing by what is generally left standing. However, Vindolanda is *en route* and it is an exceptional site. Wander through the wells and water tank to the civilian quarters and climb up the reconstructed fort (which is very authentic), as would have been seen on Hadrian's Wall. See the catapult and imagine how it was

manned and used. On the site are posts, where, if you press an *in situ* button, a recording gives information on the part of the site you are standing.

Descend to the well-laid-out gardens and enter the museum in which many fine examples of Roman antiquities are on display. For me, the well-preserved and differently designed leather shoes and

The Housesteads area of Hadrian's Wall (opposite).

Roman handwriting were fascinating. But there is much more than I can describe here, along with the necessary literature and the general information. The whole place is well appointed and has a cafeteria. Well it would have been Roman wouldn't it!

Exit the site and go right up a steep lane, then left along the minor road from Barden Mill. At Crindledykes Farm turn left and pass the buildings. For those of you who do not mind at very least, a sighting of a Charolais bull, plod on through the right of way. Otherwise to avoid its attentions, go on the road to the B6318. Reach the road either way and walk it to Housesteads car park. It is possible to reach Hadrian's Wall without visiting the museum or the fort Vercovicium, but enthusiasts will surely stop here also. The only 'attacks' on the wall nowadays are from low-flying screaming Tornado strike aircraft.

There follows a classic walk which is often bracing, along the switchbacks of the wall, with the famous view back to the clump of trees on Housesteads, in retrospect. The wall is good for a couple of kilometres, and two milecastles (guard posts), originally with turrets at mile intervals are encountered. Views of Broomlee and Greenlee Loughs are seen to the right until the wall descends to Hotbanks farm with a fine view ahead to Crag Lough which is supported by tree-crested dolerite cliffs that are occasionally used by rock climbers. The ups and downs are almost like sea cliff coastal walks. A superb milecastle and excellent views back along another good portion of wall occur within a kilometre from Crag Lough. Go over the notches of Steel Rigg and descend to Peel Cottage, noting a recently excavated section of the wall. Peel Cottage is a bunkhouse with simple accommodation. Its walls are rendered in an orangy pink, and are easily seen in any light. Finally, make your way down the lane to the hostel and visitor centre, completing a walk steeped

(Left) Towards Hotbank from above Crag Lough, Hadrian's Wall.

Milecastle No. 39, Hadrian's Wall (near Steel Rigg).

in history and bestowed with unique land-scape.

Much, much more, maybe more than your lifetime permits, awaits you on your own personal discovery of the Pennines. These hills are over 320km (200 miles) long and sometimes over 45km (30 miles) wide. This book has sampled some of the most important and best parts, in the belief that the Pennines need equal recognition to other outstanding British landscapes – if nothing else by sheer volume and variety. I sincerely hope you will discover them too!

INDEX